THE DECISION CODE

THE DECISION CODE
WHAT TO DO WHEN YOU DON'T KNOW WHAT TO DO

DR. JUSTIN MCNEIL

Copyright © 2025 Justin McNeil

All rights reserved. No part of this publication may be reproduced, distributed, or transmitted in any form or by any means, including photocopying, recording, or other electronic or mechanical methods, without the prior written permission of the publisher, except in the case of brief quotations embodied in critical reviews and certain other noncommercial uses permitted by copyright law.

Scripture quotations marked (NIV) are taken from THE HOLY BIBLE, NEW INTERNATIONAL VERSION®, NIV® Copyright © 1973, 1978, 1984, 2011 by Biblica, Inc.® Used by permission. All rights reserved worldwide.

Scripture quotations marked (ESV) are taken from the ESV® Bible (The Holy Bible, English Standard Version®), © 2001 by Crossway, a publishing ministry of Good News Publishers. ESV Text Edition: 2025. The ESV text may not be quoted in any publication made available to the public by a Creative Commons license. The ESV may not be translated in whole or in part into any other language. Used by permission. All rights reserved.

Scriptures marked (NKJV) are taken from the New King James Version®. Copyright © 1982 by Thomas Nelson. Used by permission. All rights reserved.

Cover design by Amanda C. McNeil

Interior layout by Cassie Morain

PRAISE FOR
THE DECISION CODE

"*The Decision Code is a breath of fresh air for leaders who carry the weight of big choices. It's practical, faith-filled, and deeply encouraging. I walked away with tools to navigate both everyday decisions and major crossroads, with more confidence and more surrender.*"

—**KAHLEA WADE**, ALORA SOCIETY FOUNDER AND CEO

"*Justin McNeil has cracked the code on one of life's greatest challenges. This book not only teaches you how to make decisions, it teaches you how to understand yourself in the process. Every leader, parent, and believer needs this practical wisdom. Brilliant work.*"

—**MIKE SIGNORELLI**, LEAD PASTOR, V1 CHURCH

"*I've seen firsthand how Justin lives out the wisdom in this book. The Decision Code offers clarity, insight, and practical tools for anyone feeling stuck in indecision. It's thoughtful, relatable, and deeply grounded in both psychology and real-life experience—a must-read for today's leaders.*"

—**SANDY MYERS**, PASTORAL COUNSELOR & TRAUMA-INFORMED COACH

"*The Decision Code is going to be practically helpful. Justin has figured out how to be effective at being a husband, father, friend, pastor, counselor, fitness instructor, and writer. I trust that his experience can help us make better decisions.*"

—**SALOMON DURAN**, LEAD PASTOR, CHEL CHURCH

"What Dr. Gary Chapman has done with equipping people to speak Love Languages, Dr. Justin McNeil has done to equip people with decision-making. His approach doesn't just teach you how to make decisions; it helps you tune into your own internal compass—head, heart, and gut—so that your choices align with your values, vision, and spiritual discernment. This concept is a tool you'll return to again and again. Everyone who wants to make wise, grounded decisions needs The Decision Code on their shelf."

—DR. AMANDA MCNEIL, AUTHOR, COUNSELOR, PASTOR, WIFE OF THE AUTHOR, AND COFOUNDER OF MCNEIL COACHING

"My dad has been a really good dad to me for my entire life. Whenever I'm torn between a decision, my dad will always give me tips. He reminds me I don't have to decide immediately but to take time and think about it. Even when decisions are tough and I don't know what to do, he will always help me because he's the best."

—MALACHI MCNEIL, SON OF THE AUTHOR

"Every time I've heard Dr. Justin McNeil teach, I've walked away with something I could actually use, in life and in ministry. He brings the Bible and brain science together in a way that just makes sense. This book is like sitting down with him--wise, honest, and incredibly helpful."

—DUSTIN SMITH, LEAD PASTOR OF HOPEUC NASHVILLE, FOUNDER OF HERE BE LIONS, DOVE NOMINATED SONGWRITER

"Justin McNeil lives with integrity, humility, and a deep commitment to God and family. His life of surrender gives him authority to write The Decision Code. This book is both practical and inspiring, guiding readers to build a legacy of wise decisions that honor Christ."

—AMY SMITH, SENIOR PASTOR AT CITY OF LIFE CHURCH

"Reading The Decision Code feels like spending time with Dr. McNeil himself—insightful, grounded, and deeply empowering. His rare gift for making you feel understood and equipped is felt throughout this book, which will help you quiet the noise, align your inner world, and make decisions with clarity and confidence."

—**CHRISTOPHER ALESSI**, AUTHOR AND CAMPUS PASTOR AT METRO LIFE CHURCH

"I've known Justin McNeil since he was a young man in middle school, just beginning to discover who God had called him to be. As his pastor, I've had the privilege of watching him grow into a man who deeply loves his wife, raises his son with heart, shepherds people with grace, and counsels others with a wisdom that cuts through the platitudes. His book, The Decision Code, isn't theory—it's lived truth. Every page is grounded in decades of walking with God and leading with integrity. I've seen Justin navigate life's twists and turns with steady faith, always leaning into godly wisdom to guide his steps. Reading this book feels like sitting across the table from Justin, hearing him share how to make choices that honor God and illuminate your path. I cannot recommend it enough. It is a trustworthy guide for anyone seeking to navigate the messy, beautiful journey of life."

—**DR. JEFFREY SMITH**, SENIOR PASTOR AT CITY OF LIFE CHURCH

"God has gifted Justin McNeil to bring clarity to the most common issue we face—when we don't know what to do. This book delivers a breakthrough perspective every leader needs. It aligns your head, heart, and gut to bring clarity to chaos. And I know I will be better because of this. This is a must read!"

—**NITO BEIZA**, EXECUTIVE PASTOR AT VISION CHURCH

CONTENTS

FOREWORD — 1

INTRODUCTION
DECISIONS, DECISIONS — 5

PART ONE
KNOW THYSELF — 19

CHAPTER 1
THE HEAD SIGNAL — 25

CHAPTER 2
THE HEART SIGNAL — 39

CHAPTER 3
THE GUT SIGNAL — 55

CHAPTER 4
WHERE DOES IT HURT? — 69

CHAPTER 5
KNOWING GOD — 85

PART TWO
YES, BUT... — 95

CHAPTER 6
WHEN YOUR HEAD HOLDS YOU BACK (OVERTHINKING) — 107

CHAPTER 7
WHEN YOUR HEART HOLDS YOU BACK (HURT) 117

CHAPTER 8
WHEN YOUR GUT HOLDS YOU BACK (FEAR) 129

PART THREE
NO, BUT... 141

CHAPTER 9
WHEN ONLY YOUR HEAD PUSHES YOU (APATHY) 149

CHAPTER 10
WHEN ONLY YOUR HEART PUSHES YOU (EMOTIONALISM) 161

CHAPTER 11
WHEN ONLY YOUR GUT PUSHES YOU (IMPULSIVENESS) 171

CHAPTER 12
CONCLUSION – IT'S TIME TO DECIDE 183

APPENDIX: UNDERSTANDING YOUR DECISION-MAKING STYLE 193
NOTES 216
ACKNOWLEDGEMENTS 220
ABOUT THE AUTHOR 223
RESOURCES FROM THE MCNEILS 225

FOREWORD

One of the most spiritual things that you will ever do is make a decision. Pastoring for close to fifteen years, I spend a lot of time trying to give people biblical wisdom and counsel. Most of that counsel revolves around trying to make the right decision around relationships, jobs, calling, and difficult life transitions. And we do our best to pull from scripture, conventional wisdom, discernment, and life experience. The common denominator is that most people struggle to make decisions. Yet, the ability to make decisions is probably one of the most powerful indicators of emotional, mental, and spiritual maturity and growth.

So much goes into making a decision. Evaluating the situation. Putting things in perspective. Thinking through options. Considering the impact. Mustering up the courage. And then not just making a decision, but sticking to it. Just writing that felt like a workout. But the ability to go through this process can drastically change the trajectory of your life, relationships, career, and future. I can look back on my life, and what led me to be the person I am today and to the things that I get to do was a series of decisions. Your life is a string of decisions that have mapped out a trajectory that led you to where you currently sit.

Some of us look at the decisions that we make, and it breeds confidence because we like where we are. For others, looking back at your decisions can bring shame, insecurity, or a sense of regret. If we're honest, most of us have a little bit of both. Here's the good news: Regardless of what decisions you have made in your past, the decisions that you choose to make from this point forward can radically change the direction of your life for the better. In the same way that a car headed in the wrong direction can be rerouted by a friendly GPS on our phone, you can recalculate the decisions you've made and pivot towards a better destination and a brighter future.

One thing that hindsight has taught me is that I overestimate my ability to make great decisions. In the moment, my idea always sounds like the best idea I've ever heard. Only failure, regret, and consistently bad decisions have taught me that two things need to happen. First, I need to make decisions in community and not in isolation. I need to invite trusted voices into the process of my decisions. Recently I learned about how Russian chess players throughout history have been the best in the world. Even though chess is an individual game, after a game is played, Russian chess players gather together to evaluate the decisions made on the chess board. It's my life, and I have to make my own decisions. But bringing people on the journey with me allows me to become my very best as I make the best decisions.

Making better decisions doesn't just need people; it also needs a process. The second thing I need to do is to think about how

FOREWORD

I'm making decisions. If you don't like the result of something, evaluate the method that you're using. Recently I've been learning how to play golf. The key word there is *learning*. One day I almost completely lost it and threw my club at a tree. My friend told me with a smile, "The problem isn't the stick; it's the swing." Maybe the problem isn't the cards you've been dealt, but what you've decided to do with those cards.

I think *The Decision Code* is going to help you with that. This book by my incredible friend Dr. Justin McNeil is an invitation to think about how you've been making decisions with someone who feels like the friend you always needed. Justin has walked with me through some of the toughest decisions of my entire life as a pastor, as a counselor, and as a friend. And I think after you read it, you'll see your life, your decisions, and your power to determine your future differently.

JONATHAN RIVERA
CAMPUS PASTOR, SOUTHEASTERN UNIVERSITY

INTRODUCTION

DECISIONS, DECISIONS

"Indecision steals more dreams than failure ever will."
—Danielle LaPorte

INTRODUCTION: DECISIONS, DECISIONS

WHERE do you want to eat? What do you want to do this weekend? What's your favorite movie? What's your five-year plan? Will you marry me? Do you want to have kids? Do you still love me? Should we break up? Is this the right time to launch your business? What investments are you going to make? Should you add that candidate to your team? Are you going to quit or not? Do you want us to attempt to resuscitate your loved one? To be or not to be?

Decisions can be exhausting. Just reading that first paragraph could probably make someone break out in a cold sweat. Decisions, even the small ones, create stress, and the avalanche of small decisions in life can be quite taxing. It's often speculated that we make about 35,000 decisions daily. One study found that we make 226.7 decisions a day just regarding food.[1] Maybe *that's* why I want to fight when asked about where to eat. I've already made 225.7 other food decisions that day. Give me a break.

The bigger your life, the more decisions you face. For example, technology has greatly advanced human effort, but it has also dramatically increased the number of decisions we have to make. Research shows that the average person checks their phone around ninety-six times per day, resulting in a high estimate of 5,400 clicks, swipes, or scrolls throughout the day.[2] Each one of those microdecisions adds up to an overwhelming weight.

Leaders make decisions constantly. One common estimate is that executives make around 3,500 work decisions daily, which usually end up being quite complex. A budget cut may be best for the department, but it puts a man, the sole income earner for his family, out of his job. Determining the right decision is hard when there are pros and cons at every turn.

Decision-making even burdens the youngest of us. School-aged children make around 3,000 decisions daily.³ Depending on their developmental stage, not only are they making decisions, but adults are making decisions for them, too. Perhaps you can be a little more compassionate when your child gives you one-word answers about their day after school; they're exhausted!

The small decisions certainly pile up, but the big decisions can paralyze a person for days, weeks, or even months. Think of a decision that you agonized over. How long did you wrestle with that sense of internal conflict? I guarantee no matter how long it was on the calendar, it felt much longer to your soul. The bigger the decisions, the heavier they can weigh on the heart and elicit feelings of anxiety and fear, and don't get me started on regret. One thing is clear: Decision-making demands a lot of energy from us and, as a result, can often deplete us.

Decision fatigue is the formal term for this depletion and the deteriorating quality of decisions after too much deciding. It's a phenomenon where the more choices you make, the more mentally exhausted you become, leading to poorer decisions later on. Considering how many decisions we're all making daily, that's a pretty upsetting phenomenon, isn't it?

Decision fatigue has massive consequences. One study of one thousand judicial parole decisions found that the likelihood of a favorable ruling was highest at the beginning of the day, at around 65 percent, but dropped to nearly 0 percent just before the judge's break time. After a break, the favorable decision rate would return to its peak. This suggests that decision fatigue leads to a higher likelihood of judges choosing the easier option, which in this case was denying parole.[4] In other words, always take the morning appointment at the courthouse.

Decision fatigue has been monetized in very obvious ways. Have you ever noticed the variety of products displayed in a grocery store right at the end of your shopping trip? Some call it the impulse buy section. My wife calls it "fun." One thing is for sure: You've never seen carrots or broccoli displayed at the register. It's always the brightest, sugariest, most dopamine-inducing treats. Why? Because decision fatigue confirms you're way more likely to buy something unhealthy and impulsive at the end of your shopping trip than at the beginning. Your brain is exhausted from deciding which gluten-free, low-fat, non-GMO items to get for dinner, so yeah, some Skittles or chocolate for all that hard work does sound nice.

Another study showed that decision fatigue could significantly impact financial decisions. Participants who had to make multiple decisions were more likely to choose default or easy options, such as opting for standard savings accounts rather than actively selecting investments that might yield better returns. This research suggests that decision fatigue can lead to suboptimal financial choices, which can have long-term consequences.[5]

One more example that hits home for all of us relates to how decision fatigue greatly impacts self-control. The incredible workout routine and diet you planned involve a lot of friction to initiate. You have to buy different food, decide when and how to make it, decide what sorts of workouts you will do, decide if you're in serious pain or just sore, and then decide all of this again and again. Eventually, decision fatigue sets in, and you're more prone to seek comfort, give in to temptation, and abandon the regimen because you're downright exhausted from it.

One thing is abundantly clear: There are so many decisions to make. The more we make, the more fatigued we become and the worse we become at making decisions. This frustrating reality is one of the primary reasons I took on the task of writing this book. I can't reduce the number of decisions you have to make, and I can't alleviate your present fatigue, but I can equip you with The Decision Code. This framework simplifies your decision-making by helping you confidently interpret your emotions and the signals they send you. So if all those little changes can help you make clearer, more confident decisions in moments that count, I will have accomplished my goal.

I think it's productive for me to explain a bit more about myself, as I draw a lot of the insights of this book from my experience in a few professional fields, as well as years of studying the brain and human behavior. I am an executive pastor at a vibrant and long-standing church in Central Florida. My wife, Amanda, and I are both counselors, and we own a practice that has given us the great privilege to counsel hundreds of clients. I specialize in providing counsel to individuals with sexually addictive behaviors. I also have the privilege of coaching many people in their health journey as a group fitness instructor. Finally, I'm the father to Malachi, a highly entertaining, energetic, and talented boy.

I share all of that because I hope to humanize this book for you. The fact that you'd take the time to read this is not something I take lightly, and my hope is that you'll feel personally encouraged and maybe even coached by the man behind the book. Also, I've witnessed the deepest parts of many people's decision-making processes. I've walked with people on their spiritual journey, counseled them in their mental health, coached them as they challenged their fitness, and loved and led my family within the walls of my home as we built a life together.

My combined education and experience have given me a perspective that I feel will be valuable to share with you. In the pages of this book, I'll share stories of some incredible people I've worked with in major decision points of their lives to illustrate some important truths. All names and identifying information have been changed to protect the privacy of those listed, but they've all had the option to review the portions about them, and they chose to share their story with you in this way, which I find incredibly beautiful. I hope you do, too. So you may be reading my book, but you're gleaning from the stories of many.

This is not a book about your decisions but rather how you make them. Decision-making is a skill you can refine and one our very fatigued culture desperately needs to improve. American psychologist George Weinberg put it this way: "The cure for most obstacles is, be decisive."[6] Decisiveness is a weapon to break through most obstacles in life. I've always felt decisiveness was a bit of a superpower I'm graced with, as it's one of the strongest qualities of my temperament. Decades of leadership have forced me to refine it—oftentimes the hard way. Now, I earnestly hope to help develop it in you with less difficulty.

This book is filled with thought-provoking questions because they help us learn more about ourselves. When I pose a question, feel free to pause and reflect. I'm asking because it's important, and there's no reason to blaze through the book for the sake of completion at the expense of reflection.

So, here are the first of many questions. How do you personally make decisions? Are you an external processor? Do you use a pros and cons list? Is it based on a feeling? Have you ever said YOLO? If you can start to reflect on your present decision-making process, you can also develop it further from the ideas in this book. If we really want to develop, we must be honest about where we're starting. So, be honest with yourself. How would you rate your decision-making abilities as you start on this journey with me?

If decisiveness is the cure for most obstacles, then what's the obstacle that keeps you from curing most other obstacles? It is the

INTRODUCTION: DECISIONS, DECISIONS

biggest threat to decisiveness and the prey I aim for us to hunt down together in this book: indecisiveness. Indecisiveness keeps us from making decisions and can feel like a downright war internally. Indecisiveness doesn't usually feel like the absence of a decision but rather a battle between all the possible decisions.

In counseling, one of my favorite modalities is called IFS, or Internal Family Systems. One of the guiding principles of this approach is that we are each composed of many parts. For example, one part of us wants to lose ten pounds, but another part does not want to get out of bed when the alarm goes off to exercise. One part of us wants to approach that beautiful person and ask for their phone number, but another part is terrified of how they may respond. Awareness of and compassion toward all these parts, and specifically the book *Altogether You: Experiencing Personal and Spiritual Transformation with Internal Family Systems Therapy* by Jenna Riemersma, has changed my life. It also laid the groundwork for the inspiration of this book. Simply put, I believe indecisiveness is the result of an internal argument between different parts or conflicting signals within us that contribute to our decision-making. When these signals conflict, we become frozen or frantic and are unable to decide. "I

> Indecisiveness doesn't usually feel like the absence of a decision but rather a battle between all the possible decisions.

don't know what to do" is the sound of a collision between our decision-making parts.

Decisiveness will begin to flow more easily if we can better understand these parts and negotiate that internal argument to a compromise. To understand these parts, we have to know how they work, how they react, and how they *feel* when they're activated in our bodies. I used to think decisions were simply a matter of the mind—easy explanation. But what is the mind, really? It's a bit of a lofty concept and slightly abstract, right? So many leaders are trying to develop tough-mindedness, but what is it that we're toughening? We know that the mind is the source of our consciousness or a sort of immaterial essence of our individuality. I never really had a concrete way to define the mind until my concept of it got dramatically expanded and grounded in reality. I'd like to suggest that same expansion to you.

> "I don't know what to do" is the sound of a collision between our decision-making parts.

Your mind, which may seem abstract, is the connection between three very real parts of your body: your brain, your heart, and your gut. Sit with that for a moment, because it's probably the first time you've heard the word *gut* today, but also because it's fascinating. Three parts of your physical body, and how they interplay, quite literally make up your mind. Think of it this way:

INTRODUCTION: DECISIONS, DECISIONS

Me, my wife, and our son are three individuals, yet the way we interplay is what creates a family. Yes, biology makes us related, but the kind of relationship we have is transcendent to that, and it's what creates the feeling of family between us. Three distinct entities interact in a way that brings an immaterial unit into existence. In the same way, the three components of your brain, heart, and gut interact with one another and form your mind.

Your head, heart, and gut each process decisions differently, and when they align, clarity follows. But when they contradict each other, you experience indecisiveness. Indecisiveness is not the absence of a decision but an internal battle between competing signals. You've likely experienced moments where your head says one thing, your heart another, and your gut something else entirely. The Decision Code is a method to help you decode and align these signals to make confident, wise choices without second-guessing yourself.

In this book, I'll guide you through

- understanding how your head, heart, and gut function in decision-making;
- recognizing when your signals are in conflict;
- learning when to say yes, even with uncertainty; and
- understanding when to say no, even if part of you wants to say yes.

I'm not aiming to present a new modality for counseling but rather a framework for you to implement in your day-to-day functioning. While I do implement many of these ideas in counseling clients, the goal is not another therapy, as there are too many good ones out there. Instead, I aim to give you an accessible, self-governed litmus test to aid your decision-making. I want you to know yourself so well that you can make decisions with confidence because you understand your internal conflicts.

Here's how we will hit that target together through this book. I've divided it into three parts. Part One takes a deep dive into the three different signals of decision-making: your brain, heart, and gut. To understand the strategies I'm going to equip you with, you need to first understand what's happening in all three. I'll spend some time explaining these functions and how they signal to you about a decision. Your decision-making ability is directly connected to your awareness of these three signals. The Decision Code uses these signals to your advantage for confident decision-making.

I've created a quiz for you to take that will help you understand which of these signals are more dominant, neutral, and averse in your decision-making. To be clear, we each access all three constantly, but we may assign different weights to each of them based on our individual decision-making  style. You can access this test at justincmcneil.com/quiz. Try taking it now and familiarize yourself with the results. Your decision-making style has strengths, weaknesses, and qualities that show up in all your choices. Understanding yourself gives you greater insight as to how you move through decisions. The way you move is unique, and the six decision-making styles analyzed in this quiz all move as uniquely as the pieces on a chess board. Your style is based on the how you access your signals.

Once we better understand these three signals, I will explain how trauma impacts them and inhibits our ability to see anything clearly in decision-making. While I could devote an entire book to the topic of trauma, I will contain it to one chapter strictly as it pertains to decision-making. The conclusion of Part One addresses the ways in which we can encounter the divine in these three parts of our processing. I'll share my most earnest beliefs about how God meets us, along with some biblical insights to frame them. I have structured this portion with respect to the many different kinds of readers and worldviews that may engage with this book and am confident that no matter your belief system, you'll be able to decide how to digest this portion—if at all—and still glean great value from the book.

Part Two will introduce my strategies for understanding your internal conflicts. It will explain the different kinds of conflicts we face and how they lead to our indecisiveness. I'll provide some specific ideas on how to overcome those conflicts to make swift, confident decisions. Part Two will help you know when to say yes, even if you don't feel 100 percent sure.

Part Three will focus on using the strategy of self-awareness to help you understand when *no* is the decision you should make. It will target the times when you feel confused and inclined to act against your better judgment. I'll explain why it's so hard to say no sometimes. Part Three will help you know when to say no with confidence, even if you don't feel 100 percent sure.

We've got our work cut out for us, but I'm confident that it's work worth doing. All I ask is for your honest reflection, introspection, and willingness to think differently. Again, if all this book does is make your decision-making a little less difficult, it will be a huge improvement, since you'll make billions of decisions in your lifetime. If you're ready and still interested, let's move into Part One so you can gain a deeper understanding of your mind. If you're not ready or no longer interested, then maybe it's a good time to put this down and go get some food. By the way, where do you want to eat?

PART ONE

KNOW THYSELF

"Knowing yourself is the beginning of all wisdom."
—Aristotle

PART ONE: KNOW THYSELF

HAVE you ever been in your car, miles from home, when suddenly you realize you've been driving on autopilot? You've made all the correct turns, stopped at the right lights, and navigated traffic, but you have zero recollection of doing any of it. Your body knew exactly what to do while your mind was somewhere else entirely.

That same autopilot mode often governs our decisions. We make choices, sometimes life-altering, without really understanding what's driving them. We go with our gut, follow our heart, or use our head, but rarely do we stop to question why we're favoring one signal over the others or what each is really telling us. This is why truly knowing yourself is the essential first step in mastering The Decision Code.

In the pages ahead, we will explore the three primary signals that guide every decision you make: your head, your heart, and your gut. Each of these signals has its own wisdom, its own perspective, and its own blind spots. Each speaks a slightly different language and needs to be understood if you want to make decisions with confidence and clarity.

Your head signal is the voice of logic and reason. It analyzes data, weighs options, and forecasts outcomes. It's the part of you that creates spreadsheets, reads reviews before purchasing, and thinks through consequences. But as powerful as this signal is, logic alone cannot guide your life's most meaningful choices.

Your heart signal is the voice of emotion and connection. It tells you what matters, what brings joy, and what aligns with your deepest values. It's the part of you that falls in love, feels compassion for others, and knows when something resonates at a soul level. But emotions, while essential, can sometimes cloud judgment if not balanced with other inputs.

Your gut signal is the voice of intuition and instinct. It's that immediate, visceral knowing that something is right or wrong before you can explain why. It's the part of you that senses danger, recognizes opportunity, and knows when to act quickly. But instincts, while powerful, can sometimes be reactive rather than responsive if not tempered with reflection.

Together, these three signals form the navigation system for your life. When they align, decisions feel clear and confident. When they conflict, you experience the frustrating paralysis of indecision.

Beyond understanding these signals individually, we'll also explore how past trauma can distort them, causing what should be clear signals to become painful aches that hold you back rather than guide you forward. We'll learn how to distinguish between signals that drive us toward growth and aches that keep us stuck in patterns of protection.

For those whose faith is central to their lives, we'll also explore how God speaks through these signals: how divine wisdom can illuminate our understanding, divine love can heal our hearts, and divine guidance can clarify our instincts. This spiritual dimension isn't separate from our decision-making process; it's woven throughout it, offering depth and perspective to every choice we face.

As we begin this exploration, I'd encourage you to approach these chapters with genuine curiosity about yourself. The goal isn't just to absorb information but to better understand how you personally experience these signals. Notice which signal tends to dominate your decisions. Pay attention to which one you tend to ignore or discount. Reflect on times when these signals have led you well and times when they've led you astray.

The questions at the end of each chapter are invitations to deeper self-awareness. Take time with them. Journal your responses. Discuss them with people who know you well. The more honesty and reflection you bring to this process, the more valuable it will be.

Before we can apply The Decision Code to the choices we face, we need to understand the language of our internal signals. We need to recognize their distinct voices, appreciate their unique wisdom, and learn how they're meant to work together. We need to uncover the distortions that might be affecting how we receive and interpret these signals. In short, we need to know ourselves.

So let's begin with the signal that might seem most straightforward but often proves surprisingly complex: the head signal. Once you understand how your brain, that remarkable universe between your ears, influences your life, you'll realize how frequently the head signal shows up in your life.

CHAPTER 1

THE HEAD SIGNAL

"Nothing in the world is more dangerous than sincere ignorance and conscientious stupidity."
—Martin Luther King Jr.

I want you to think of the best superhero of all time, and then I'll tell you why you're wrong if you're thinking of anyone other than Dr. Strange. This is not even up for debate. He not only has arguably the most power of any hero, but he has honed the most control over it. He can manipulate time and space, and most importantly, his cape fights, too. He's a character that I resonate with so deeply that I often have to remind myself I'm Justin McNeil, not Stephen Strange. I can hear my non-geek readers groaning at me, but I have to believe some out there know what it's like to see yourself in a superhero. It doesn't help that on two different birthdays I was given a custom rendering of me as Dr. Strange by two different animators. Admittedly, I like to think of them as hyper-realistic portraits, including the swirling superpowers.

Not only is Dr. Strange incredibly powerful, but the human side of his origin story grips me. He is a brilliant neurosurgeon who studies and understands the brain in exceptional ways. A tragic accident damages his manual functioning and sets him on a quest to unlock the use of his brain to heal his injuries. The journey becomes quite fantastic as he discovers his potential for healing and the untold power he can wield.

I've never felt more like Dr. Strange than while chaperoning one of my son's field trips to a science center. I like to think of this as my superhero origin story. One exhibit at the science center that day was specifically about the brain and neurofeedback technology. Filled with curiosity, I sat down and hooked myself up to an electroencephalogram. This machine, the EEG, is strapped around the head and, through fine-tuned sensors, can detect the change of electrical activity in the brain. The primary brain waves monitored by an EEG are typically alpha and theta waves, which are usually associated with relaxation.

In other words, this machine can detect how well the subject's brain is relaxed on an electrical level. The EEG was connected to a simple machine that received the input and powered a fan, which blew an airstream into a small plastic tube with a ping-pong ball in it. So if I was able to relax my brain, I could power the machine and essentially control the floating ping-pong ball through the tube, moving it to whatever height I desired. It's surprisingly not easy to relax when there's a flashing timer on the screen, a clearly marked line for the ball to pass, and a class full of six-year-olds standing around you. No matter the pressure, though, true heroes always rise up, and so did that ping-pong ball. I marveled as it hovered higher when I calmed myself and dipped when I lost focus. For those few seconds, I felt like I was saving the world by controlling that ping-pong ball, and my son was convinced I had superpowers, too.

I can't quite put into words how fascinating and downright magical it felt to watch that ball rise by the power of my brain, but I'll never forget it. Brain-computer interfacing has a massive frontier of development, with companies like Neuralink documenting a case involving a paralyzed man with a spinal cord injury who was able to control a robotic arm and even walk using a brain implant that bypassed the damaged spinal cord. You can imagine my excitement when I heard that based on how I reacted to a ping-pong ball.

The brain houses approximately one hundred billion neurons, each intricately connected through synapses that transmit signals using various neurotransmitters. These neurons, along with a complex network of hormones and other chemical messengers, work together to regulate every aspect of thought, emotion, and bodily function. The brain is like a supercomputer constantly at work within us. Before the development of brain imaging technology in the late twentieth century, scientists had not been able to study the inner workings of the living brain. However, technology has now permitted researchers to observe what occurs within the brain as a person is thinking, feeling, and experiencing external stimulation. This research has opened up the discussion in a way that was previously not possible. It is now understood that the brain is both sensitive to external stimulation and powerful in dictating human behavior. Admittedly, the brain is my favorite topic of the many I'll discuss in this book, so humor me as we briefly examine some of the most important facts about it.

What is known about the brain is dwarfed by what is not known. Science is only now beginning to uncover the fascinating capacity the brain possesses. However, even with the developments that have come about, there is still much to be learned about our understanding of the brain. First and foremost, the brain is an organ. It has physical components and functions that have physical results. It's tricky because you don't see your brain, so it's easy to forget it as a physical organ. These physical dynamics can end up affecting the emotions and immaterial aspects of your mind and spirit, but it is crucial to first observe the brain as the physical organ that it is. The many regions of the brain dictate various functions and behaviors.

For example, one of the most important regions of the brain is the prefrontal cortex (PFC). It is located in the frontal lobe and is the region of the brain that regulates logical thinking, planning for the future, control of behavior, and the possibility for compassion to occur between individuals. Though there is not one region of the brain that is inherently more "good" than another, if there were a proverbial angel and devil perched on a person's shoulders, the angel might just be the PFC. When the PFC works properly, people are thoughtful, empathic, compassionate, able to appropriately express their feelings, organized, and goal directed. They are no longer driven by pure instincts to desire the here and now but rather can control impulses and direct behavior in a positive direction for the long term.[1]

Not surprisingly, a damaged or unhealthy PFC leads to quite the opposite results. Without the governing restraint that this region provides, people can become reactive and reckless with their behavior. Individuals with poor PFC function do not seem to be able to draw on their past experiences, and they react impulsively to satisfy their immediate wants and needs.[2] It is sobering to think that many people who have been disregarded as foolish or hedonistic could actually be dealing with a physical issue rather than merely a moral one. This is not to dismiss personal responsibility but rather to illuminate possibilities for how we can better navigate challenges.

Another critical region of the brain is the limbic system. Located deep within the brain's temporal lobes, the limbic system is the source of our most primal and emotional responses. The limbic system can be seen as the little devil perched on the shoulder of a person. It is the region where emotion, fear, passion, impulse, and self-centeredness are born. Again, this is not inherently "bad," as emotion is an integral part of the human experience. For example, without some degree of fear, one would not survive danger very long. When the temporal lobes and deep limbic system work right, people have a good sense of personal history or memory, are even-keeled in emotions, have access to spiritual experiences, and have control over their temper. When there are problems in these parts of the brain, people's memories suffer. They either lack spiritual experience or have destructive ones, and they experience mood swings and tempers that are out of control.[3]

These regions of the brain are in a constant state of shaping and reshaping themselves in response to the stimuli provided by experiences and thoughts. This constant change is called neuroplasticity, which is the ability of the human brain to structurally rearrange itself in response to a wide variety of positive and negative effects.[4] This is why everything from diet and exercise to media consumption matters so much. Every single stimulus in your life has the capacity to shape your brain and should be treated as such. The discovery that the outside world is the brain's real food is intriguing. The brain encompasses everything you see, read, hear, and watch, and is regularly being shaped and reshaped by the information you take in. If that doesn't make you want to put your phone down a little more often, I don't know what will.

> **The brain encompasses everything you see, read, hear, and watch, and is regularly being shaped and reshaped by the information you take in.**

Even though this information may have felt dense, it's only a fraction of what could be said about the brain. Countless authors and scientists, far more qualified than I, have produced incredible insights into the brain and how it impacts every aspect of our lives. I want to focus specifically on how the brain shows up in our decision-making process. The brain helps us know what to do by generating an informant I like to call the head signal.

Think about your drive home from work. How long does this drive take at five o'clock on Friday? How long would it take at eleven o'clock in the morning on Saturday? What's the most convenient stop for food on the way? All of these questions stimulate your head. You know these answers because you've observed the information and can deduce the best possible response. It's clear *how* you know this, but I want you to pay attention to *where* you know this. It's a signal that comes from—and I need you to visualize me tapping my finger on your temple rhythmically with these next two words for this to work—*right here.* This is the head signal.

The head signal is something you develop through the gathering of knowledge. For example, the podcast you listened to, the class you took, the book you read, the video you watched, and the speech you heard all contributed to your head signal. It's really hard to make good decisions if you're not making *informed* decisions. Information gathering is a primary component of this.

Another way that the head signal is strengthened is through observation. Watching a skill demonstrated before you and observing its nuances helps you understand it cognitively, even if you've never attempted it yourself. Extreme couponing is a skill I'll never quite be able to make sense of. Certainly you've seen the social media posts where, somehow, someone went into the grocery store with two dollars and a binder of coupons and emerged with forty-seven tubes of toothpaste, sixteen bottles of detergent, and a sixty-dollar profit. I remember this kind of couponing being such a craze that a woman at our church hosted a small group so that other women could watch and learn her ways. She was giving others a chance to observe and increase their knowledge, as well as their toothpaste inventory.

One additional and important way we develop the head signal is through data. How much money is in the account? How much do I weigh? How long has the house been on the market? How many layoffs are happening? What are the side effects of this treatment? All of these questions are ways of gathering data, which increases knowledge and can help with the decision-making process. Data helps clarify what is and isn't true in a decision. My friend, Matt, is a business coach and strategist. He is constantly reminding me of the importance of data-driven decisions. Leaders who "feel" that things are going well may not realize that the numbers tell a different story. Conversely, reactive alarm over something that feels bad may not be necessary when the data shows revenue and growth are on an upward trend. Matt can shut down almost any spiraling thought (and has for me many times) with some cold-hard data. Without data, we are missing a huge component of our head signal.

> **Without data, we are missing a huge component of our head signal.**

The head signal is one of the ways we *know* what to do, and even though it's not the only way, it's an important one. The head signal shows up in decision-making first and foremost through logical reasoning. It sounds like, "What makes the most sense in this situation?" You can *feel* your head signal showing up in your decision-making when trying to rationalize, streamline, and make things more efficient. The head signal feels like you're governing over the details of the decision, and your inner adult is adulting really hard to achieve the best possible outcome.

In addition to reasoning, the head signal often looks like forecasting, which is projecting how decisions will unfold. If I decide to relocate for this job, my life will go through the following changes. If x, then y. The brain works overtime to help us run scenarios, forecast potential outcomes, and determine what will happen. Studies estimate that 30–50 percent of our waking thoughts involve "mental time travel," where we either reflect on the past or anticipate the future. This includes daydreaming, planning, worrying, and simulating future events.[5] A significant portion of our head signal is based on forecasting and preparing for future decisions, indicating that anticipation is a natural and constant part of our decision-making process.

Risk assessment is the final way that our head signal manifests in decision-making. Whether this is the age-old pros and cons list or a rigorous cost-benefit analysis, risk assessment is something we do from our head. You'll even notice when you're considering the risk of a decision that your eyebrows furrow, you may feel the urge to rub your forehead, and it seems like your brain is in overdrive. Your head is trying to compute data, observations, reason, and risk to aid in the decision-making process.

Now that we've fully inspected the nature of the head signal on a biological level, how it's developed, and how it shows up, it's time for you to take a moment and reflect on it. Based on your quiz scores and self-reflection, how dominant is your head signal in decision-making? Are you governed totally by reason and attempt to strip emotion from your decisions? Or does your head seem to shut down when faced with a big decision while you struggle to be rational?

Usually the person who is head-dominant in decision-making has the following strengths:

- data-driven
- rational
- logical
- methodical

The weaknesses of the head-dominant person can appear as the following:

- pride
- overthinking
- lack of action
- callousness

If you naturally operate from a very head-dominant posture in life, you may view it as supreme. This is definitely one signal from which I often operate, so it's easy to feel like it's the best way to process. However, I've learned the hard way that it's not any more important than the other signals within us. If you're like me, though, maybe you can relate to being very head-heavy in decision-making. Decisions sound like they bounce around in my actual, physical head. When I'm making a decision, I think about it with very little emotion, hoping that by the power of thought I'll be able to move my life like I moved that ping-pong ball. As we'll soon discover, though, thinking isn't the only way to approach a decision. It's just one of three equal parts. Before we move on, I'd like for you to take some time and engage with personal reflection on the topic of head signals.

PERSONAL REFLECTIONS – THE HEAD SIGNAL

1. Considering my Decision Code quiz results, am I head-dominant or not? If so, how do I identify with the Architect or Strategist style?
2. What decision in my life right now needs more information, observation, or data?
3. What was one of my best rational decisions?
4. What am I most actively forecasting and assessing risks about currently?

CHAPTER 2

THE HEART SIGNAL

"The heart has its reasons of which reason knows nothing."
—Blaise Pascal

I have a lot of fond memories from growing up as an only child. My parents were always so kind and generous to me. I remember being fascinated by bunk beds and thought I would never get the joy of sleeping on a top bunk. One day, my mom surprised me with a bunk bed with a regular bed on the top and a futon couch on the bottom. You've never seen a kid happier to climb a ladder to bed. My parents also noticed the phase of my childhood when I became obsessed with space. They got a stencil to cover my bedroom ceiling, and Dad painted glow-in-the-dark stars in accurate positions of the night sky. Those stars still shine every night in what is now my son's room at their house, and when he visits them, he falls asleep looking at the same glow I did almost thirty years ago.

Perhaps the fondest memory of all, though, was Christmas morning. Each year I would eagerly await the chance to come out of my bedroom and see the presents surrounding the tree. I would hardly ever sleep, and to be honest with you, I still don't sleep well on Christmas Eve out of sheer excitement. Growing up, I got some pretty amazing gifts, like a pinball machine and a Nintendo. My parents are rather quiet and reserved people, but they have a very loud son. One year they even got me a karaoke machine. I'm not sure how much sacrificial love it must've taken for them to give me something that made me louder, but it's a special kind of love.

I can still remember the karaoke machine. Since this was before we could play unlimited music from our phones, it was pretty impressive that this machine could strike up hundreds of different songs, their lyrics, *and* some digitized harmonies that layered on top of your voice. It's how I learned important pieces of music like NSYNC's "Bye Bye Bye" and Aerosmith's "I Don't Wanna Miss a Thing." Eventually, one of the buttons on the machine broke, and I could only play one song: Celine Dion's "My Heart Will Go On." In this case, it went on and on and on.

"Near, far, wherever you are, I believe that the heart does go on." It's okay if you need a second to belt it out. If my karaoke machine had to be stuck on one song, I wasn't mad about it being that one. It's a full-on anthem about the power of the heart, and when you hear Celine sing it, you can *feel* it in your chest.

That feeling, that location in your body, is the epicenter of the heart signal. The heart is a vital part of the body to understand, as it contributes greatly to decision-making. I once heard the heart described as the most unique and powerful electromagnet on earth. It's constantly emitting magnetic energy that can attract or repel others.

The heart, a muscular organ about the size of a fist, is the powerhouse of our circulatory system, tirelessly pumping blood to sustain every cell in the body. It's more than just a mechanical pump. It's a vital communication hub that interacts intimately with the brain and the rest of the body. The heart contains approximately forty thousand neurons, often referred to as "heart neurons" or intrinsic cardiac neurons. They play a crucial role in regulating heart function and can communicate with the brain.[1]

For centuries, the heart has been revered not only as a life-sustaining organ but also as the symbolic seat of emotions and spirit. In recent years, science has begun to explore this connection more deeply, revealing that the heart plays a far more intricate role in our lives than we might have imagined. As we delve into the fascinating dynamics of this organ, I invite you to critically consider the power of your heart in your decision-making.

It's easy to think of the heart merely as a pump, but it's important to remember that it is also a sensory organ with its own intrinsic nervous system, sometimes referred to as the "heart brain." This network allows the heart to process information, make decisions, and even influence our emotions. The heart's ability to send signals to the brain, affecting everything from cognitive function to emotional state, suggests that it plays a significant role in shaping our experiences. Understanding the heart as a physical and emotional organ can help us better navigate the challenges we face in health and our daily lives.

One of the most remarkable regions of the heart is the sinoatrial (SA) node, often called the heart's natural pacemaker. Located in the right atrium, the SA node is responsible for setting the rhythm of the heart's contractions, ensuring that blood is efficiently circulated throughout the body. But the heart's influence extends beyond mere mechanics. Research has shown that heart rhythms can reflect our emotional states, with coherence in heart rate variability (HRV) associated with positive emotions such as love, appreciation, and compassion. When our heart rhythms are harmonious, we experience greater emotional stability, mental clarity, and overall well-being. In a sense, the heart's rhythm is like the conductor of an orchestra, coordinating the symphony of bodily functions and emotional experiences.

On the flip side, when the heart is under stress, whether due to physical strain, unhealthy lifestyle choices, or emotional turmoil, the effects can be profound. A heart that beats erratically or struggles to maintain its rhythm can lead to a cascade of negative outcomes, from increased anxiety and cognitive fog to serious health conditions like heart disease. Many of the stressors we dismiss as mere annoyances can have a tangible impact on our heart's function and, by extension, our overall health. Yet, by paying attention to the signals our heart sends, we can learn to manage stress more effectively, improving not only our physical health but also our emotional resilience.

The heart's constant interaction with the brain and body is a testament to its complexity and importance. This dynamic interplay, often referred to as heart-brain coherence, underscores the idea that the heart is not merely a passive organ but an active participant in our lives. The discovery that the heart can influence emotions, thoughts, and behaviors adds a new dimension to how we understand ourselves. It reminds us that caring for our heart involves more than just physical maintenance. It requires an awareness of how our emotions, thoughts, and actions shape the very rhythm of our lives. Every heartbeat is a reminder that the heart is not just at the center of our circulatory system but at the core of our experience as human beings. If anything, this knowledge should inspire us to lead heart-healthy lives.

The heart signal isn't something we know in our head. It's something we feel in our chest. It may not be information-based, but it's a profound signal nonetheless. Imagine being away from your children or loved ones for some time. If I asked you whether or not you missed them, the answer wouldn't require you to look at a calendar and determine how long it's been. Your chest would answer with a resounding signal of how much you missed them. I'm currently writing this sentence while on a plane heading home to see my son after eight days away. I don't need my head to tell me how hard I'm going to hug that kid as soon as I see him. My heart has already determined it.

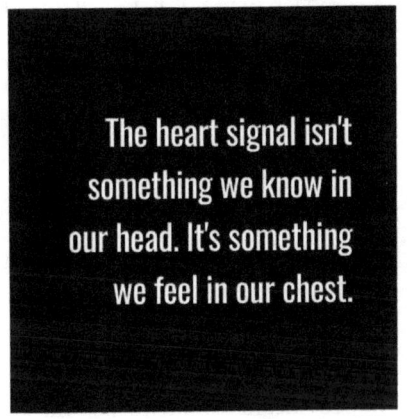

The heart signal is something we develop in multiple ways, but the primary way is through our emotions. If heart signals were a beautiful painting, emotions would be the individual jars of paint colors sitting in front of the canvas. In my counseling work, I spend a lot of time interacting with emotions. One thing I've learned is that most people have a habit of apologizing for their emotions. I observe a frequent tendency to think emotions are weaknesses, and tears are a sign of immaturity. I, however, view emotions as messengers. They're always trying to tell us something, and they're always contributing to our heart signal.

Think of your emotions as indicators on a car's dashboard. Sometimes when those signals light up, we know exactly what they mean. The gas tank light tells me I need to refuel soon. But my wife's philosophy is that we have plenty of time, at least fifty more miles. The low tire pressure indicator informs me I need to address a leak soon. But not every signal is so clear if you're unfamiliar with them. What do those squiggly lines mean behind the car? Why does that signal say ABS? Unfamiliar signals can lead to more confusion rather than the necessary action.

In the same way, emotions pop up in our hearts because they're meant to incite action. Joy tells us we want more of whatever is happening. Pain tells us we need something to stop. Sadness is the emotion that tells us something really matters to us. Anger tells us we need change. If we're not really in tune with our emotions, however, we can easily respond to them poorly. Instead of letting anger drive us to change, we can let it drive us to rage, which usually doesn't change things for the better. Instead of recognizing the depth of meaning that sadness reveals, we can feel compelled to numb it or distract ourselves from it.

Emotions are the informants of the heart signal. If you've never watched *Inside Out* and *Inside Out 2*, I think they do a beautiful job of illustrating how emotions can all work together, and sometimes not at all. If we really want to understand ourselves on a heart level, we must become well attuned to our emotions. We need to learn how to radically feel what is happening within us and how to label it, express it, and process it. This can happen with the help of a journaling practice, emotional intimacy with a loved one, and a good counselor. The more in tune you are with your emotions, the more you can access your heart signal.

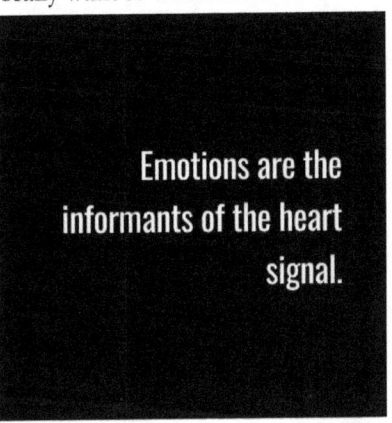

Another way we develop the heart signal is through relationships. The fascinating electromagnet beating within your chest is wired for relationships with others. Relationships change us in a profound way. We start to think, act, and talk like the people we relate with most often. We also develop deep-rooted sentiments on life based on our relationships. When I was young and watched the Olympics, I never quite understood why the camera would cut to the parents of the athletes so often or why said parents were squirming in their seats with every stunt, weeping so often, and screaming so much. Now, having a child of my own, nothing in the Olympics moves me more than those moments. Even though I may not understand what those parents are going through from my head, having never cheered my son through an Olympic game, I know what they're feeling from my heart. The power of relationships is something that lodges deep in our hearts. The heart signal is how we know what it's like to love deeply, feel jealousy, have a sick child, feel attraction, win and lose.

One other way the heart signal is developed is through inspiration. This one is a little elusive, but it cannot be overlooked. You know the feeling that sparks within you when your heart feels as if it's going to leap out of your chest. Inspiration can show up as the proverbial love at first sight when you're inspired by a person's appearance or presence. It can also look like seeing someone perform a skill artistically or athletically and feeling the newfound inspiration to develop that quality within yourself. It can even look like hearing a song that taps an emotion in you that flows out through tears. Inspiration is an unexpected yet profound way that the heart signal is crafted.

The heart signal shows up in decision-making very differently from the head signal. Whereas the head signal shows up as reasoning, forecasting, and risk assessment, the heart signal follows a different pathway completely. The first way the heart signal shows up in decision-making is through feelings. I need to distinguish this a bit from emotions. Emotions are indicators of what's going on within us, but feelings are heart-based conclusions about what's going on around us. *I feel like I shouldn't tell my friends about what happened. I feel like getting a new hairstyle will help me get over my ex. I feel like this is too much pressure for me.* Feelings are fueling most people's decisions without them even realizing it.

How we feel about a decision is usually rooted in how we feel about ourselves. For example, a more confident person may see risk as another opportunity to win, while a more insecure person feels like they'll be embarrassed yet again. The thing about feelings is you don't always realize they're coming from within you because they seem so true. I once had a professor who prohibited anyone in the class from using the phrase "I feel" during our discussions and debates. It was hilarious how many times we had to stop ourselves because most arguments were based entirely on feelings. I became a pro at using the phrase "Something within me says" as a substitute for "I feel." It's vital to recognize your feelings in a decision because otherwise, they're steering you without you even realizing it.

> **How we feel about a decision is usually rooted in how we feel about ourselves.**

Another way that the heart signal shows up in decision-making is through passion. You may know something from your head, but passion adds intensity to it, like a **bold font** adds intensity to a sentence. Whether you're passionate about a particular sport, an artist, a location, a food, or a person, the very mention of that topic incites passion in you. Passion shapes our heart signal by steering us toward what moves us most. Sometimes it's unexplainable, but passion adds intensity to the signal that comes from deep within your heart.

One last way that the heart signal infuses our decisions is through desire. The heart tells us what it wants. Our desires are powerful agents of decision-making. Sometimes we desire things that are good for us; other times we desire far more destructive options. Regardless, desire often tips the scale in decision-making. When you feel an intense pull in a specific direction, it's probably worth exploring your heart to see how and why desire is affecting your decision.

Having thoroughly studied the heart in this chapter, my hope is that you have a deeper appreciation for the weight it carries in your functioning and decision-making. If you're a person who is more heart-dominant and who responds to the heart signal most frequently, you probably often feel your way through decisions. You have an incredible way of letting your emotions, relationships, and inspirations guide you in making decisions. I genuinely find my heart-dominant friends to be a breath of fresh air because it's the signal I naturally turn to last.

The heart-dominant individual brings the following strengths to decision-making:

- passion/intensity
- awareness of relational impact
- sensitivity

Meanwhile, the weaknesses of the heart-dominant person can look like the following:

- bitterness
- irrationality
- inconsistency
- people-pleasing

If you tend to operate more from your heart signal, you have probably been well aware of this for some time. Your decisions feel like choices that come from your heart but can also feel a little chaotic. Sometimes your feelings take you one way, but then they quickly change. Even though you haven't always made the most rational decisions, your ability to bring emotion, care, and empathy to your decisions is powerful. I salute you, my heart-dominant friends. I believe the heart will go on.

SIGNAL COMPARISON CHART

	HEAD SIGNAL	HEART SIGNAL
PRIMARY VOICE	Logic & Analysis	Emotions & Connection
DEVELOPED THROUGH	Knowledge, observation, data	Relationships, emotions, inspiration
SOUNDS LIKE...	"What makes the most sense?"	"How do I feel about this?"
SHOWS UP AS	• Reasoning & rationalization • Forecasting outcomes • Risk assessment • Pros & cons lists	• Feelings about situations • Emotional responses • Relational insights • What matters deeply
STRENGTH	Clarity, structure, objectivity	Passion, meaning, authenticity
GROWTH OPPORTUNITY	Analysis paralysis, overthinking	Emotional flooding, hurt-based hesitation
TRUST IT WHEN	You need facts & strategic planning	You need to honor what matters most
QUESTION IT WHEN	You're stuck in endless loops	Past pain is clouding judgment

PERSONAL REFLECTIONS – THE HEART SIGNAL

1. Considering my Decision Code quiz results, am I heart-dominant or not? If so, how do I identify with the Empath or Intuitive style?
2. What decision in my life right now would benefit from more emotion, relationship, and inspiration?
3. What was one decision in my life that brought up the biggest emotions?
4. What am I currently doing that sparks the most passion in me?

CHAPTER 3

THE GUT SIGNAL

"There is more wisdom in your body than in your deepest philosophy."
—Friedrich Nietzsche

I'M a generally energetic person with a naturally happy demeanor. I enjoy having fun and connecting with people. There is, however, one very real threat to this usual state. In the same way you wouldn't like Bruce Banner when he's angry, you wouldn't like me when I'm *hangry*. Hangry is my self-diagnosed state of anger triggered by hunger, and it is Hulk-like in its power.

I once spoke at an event out of town and was excited to spend time with friends I don't normally get to see. The event started in the morning and went past lunchtime. Despite my better judgment, I decided to wait to eat until almost four o'clock that afternoon with my friends. The first few minutes of the car ride to the restaurant were filled with laughter and conversations, but then I started to feel awful. I texted my wife, who was in the car with us, that I thought I might have the flu or covid because my body felt like it was shutting down. My friend noticed I was suddenly not doing well, and the whole mood in the car shifted.

When we finally arrived at the restaurant, I took my first bite of food and had almost a miraculous turnaround. I was right back to laughing and leading the conversation. No flu. No covid. Just hangry. To this day, my friend makes sure I've eaten so he never has to see me like that again. No one has had to endure the brunt of this more than my wife. If my stomach is empty, so is my tolerance. My patience? Gone. My ability to engage in rational discussion? Depleted. My kindness? Withering away, one minute at a time. My wife has learned, with the wisdom of a seasoned warrior, that there is a simple rule in our household: Don't bring up anything important if Justin hasn't eaten.

She has tested this rule in the past, and the results were conclusive. A minor disagreement about weekend plans suddenly felt like an all-out ideological war. A question about budgeting was met with an impassioned, illogical speech about the foolishness of spending.

And yet, the moment food enters my system, I transform. It's like watching a glitchy computer suddenly restart. My mood stabilizes, my perspective clears, and I can once again operate like a functional adult. This is a dynamic and perhaps dramatic display of the gut signal.

We tend to assume that decisions come from our heads and that our brains are the central processing units of all wisdom, logic, and decision-making. But any person who has ever made a bad choice out of hunger, exhaustion, or pure instinct knows that the gut plays a role, too.

The gut signal is the body's intuitive wisdom, developed through a combination of biology, experience, and immediate bodily responses. It is the signal that doesn't require deep thought, debate, or deliberation; it just *is*. It's why you feel an instinctual sense of danger in certain situations, why you get a literal *gut feeling* about a person, and why your mood is different when you're running on an empty stomach.

> The phrase "trust your gut" is more than just a motivational cliché; it's rooted in neuroscience and physiology.

The phrase "trust your gut" is more than just a motivational cliché; it's rooted in neuroscience and physiology. The gut, also known as the enteric nervous system (ENS), contains over one hundred million neurons, earning it the nickname "the second brain." These neurons don't just control digestion; they also send signals to the brain that influence mood, decision-making, and even social behavior.

We develop the gut signal in three key ways: food, instincts, and needs.

Science confirms what my wife already knows: Hunger affects mood, judgment, and decision-making. One study published in *Psychopharmacology* found that low blood sugar levels increase impulsivity and aggression, reinforcing the idea that an empty stomach can quite literally make us behave differently.[1] Similarly, research from Ohio State University found that spouses with lower blood sugar levels were more likely to lash out at their partners, proving that *hanger* is a very real phenomenon.[2]

But food's impact on our gut signal goes beyond hanger. The gut-brain connection, often called the gut-brain axis, is one of the most fascinating discoveries in neuroscience and nutrition. The gut produces 95 percent of the body's serotonin, the neurotransmitter responsible for regulating mood, emotions, and even social behavior.[3]

This means that what we eat directly influences not just our bodies but our mental clarity, emotional stability, and decision-making abilities. A diet high in processed foods and sugar can contribute to anxiety and impulsivity, while a diet rich in whole foods, fiber, and healthy fats supports better emotional regulation and cognitive function.

So yes, eating a nutritious meal might actually help you make better life choices. (Or, at the very least, prevent you from getting into a full-blown existential crisis over why your Wi-Fi is running slow.) I won't attempt to overstep my bounds, as there are plenty of gifted nutritionists and dietitians who could better explain this. Still, it would be ignorant for me not to include food as one of the most significant contributing factors to how we think, feel, and ultimately decide.

Have you ever walked into a room and immediately felt uncomfortable? Or met someone and, for no logical reason, felt like something was "off"? That's the gut signal at work. Instincts are not random. They are the product of a complex system of self-preservation, finely tuned to help us survive. These gut instincts send a signal to the amygdala, often referred to as the brain's "fear center," which processes threats in milliseconds, long before the rational part of the brain (the PFC) has time to catch up.

One study showed that people can detect fear in someone else's body language even before they are consciously aware of it.[4]

This means that your gut picks up on subtle cues, such as body language, tone, and micro-expressions that your conscious brain hasn't yet registered. While instincts aren't always right, they often provide critical information that logic alone might miss. The trick is learning when to trust them and when to pause and evaluate further.

One final way we develop the gut signal is through our needs. The body has an incredible way of communicating what it needs if we're paying attention. Dehydration? You'll feel sluggish. Lack of sleep? You'll be irritable and foggy-headed. Overworked? You'll feel drained and disengaged.

Sleep deprivation significantly weakens decision-making abilities, particularly in high-stakes situations.[5] When basic physiological or emotional needs go unmet, higher-level thinking (like long-term planning or moral reasoning) takes a backseat. This is why the gut signal is often most evident when we are deprived of something like food, rest, or emotional connection. Our decisions change because our needs dictate our perspective.

The gut signal influences how we judge, respond to urges, and find motivation. It plays a crucial role in how we judge people, situations, and risks. Whether it's a split-second assessment of a stranger, a hunch about a business opportunity, or the immediate *nope* you feel when walking into a sketchy situation, the gut acts as a rapid decision-making tool.

People form first impressions of a stranger's trustworthiness in less than a tenth of a second.[6] This means that before we even realize it, our gut has already cast a vote on whether someone is safe, competent, or likable. While gut judgments are not always correct, they are often based on subconscious pattern recognition, like tiny cues in body language, tone, and behavior that our rational brain has not yet processed.

If the gut signal had a voice, urges would be its loudest expression. Unlike the quiet, observational nature of instincts, urges are immediate, visceral, and demanding. They arise as intense cravings for action, whether it's eating a specific food, making an impulsive purchase, sending a risky text, or abandoning work mid-task to scroll through social media.

Urges exist because our body is constantly seeking balance. If we are deficient in something, be it nutrients, rest, dopamine, or connection, our gut signal fires up in the form of an urge. However, urges can be misleading. The body craves sugar when it's low on energy, but that doesn't mean devouring a dozen donuts is the best solution. We may feel the urge to lash out when stressed, but that doesn't mean acting on it will resolve anything.

Intense food cravings are often driven by emotional and psychological triggers, not by actual nutritional deficits.[7] This is why we rarely crave a balanced meal, and instead reach for comfort foods high in sugar, fat, or salt. The same principle applies beyond food: Our urges may not always point to what we *actually* need but rather to what brings the fastest relief.

This is why self-awareness is crucial when responding to urges. The first step is learning to pause before acting. When an urge arises, ask yourself the following questions:
- What is this urge trying to solve?
- Is this a short-term fix or a long-term solution?
- Is there a healthier way to meet this need?

Understanding the science of urges also helps us build better habits. Replacing an unhealthy response with a constructive alternative is more effective than simply trying to suppress the urge.[8] If stress triggers an urge to overeat, replacing the response with deep breathing or physical movement can help shift the behavior over time.

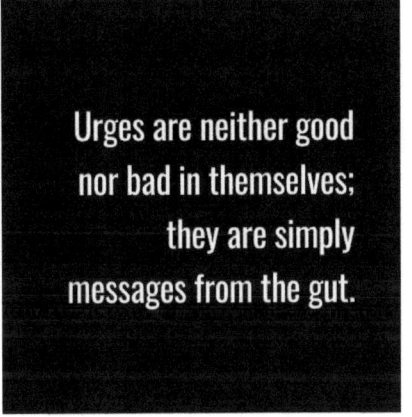

Urges are neither good nor bad in themselves; they are simply messages from the gut. Learning to interpret them wisely empowers us to act intentionally rather than impulsively.

If urges are the immediate pull toward action, motivation is the long-term drive that sustains our decisions over time. Motivation is often thought of as a function of the brain, but research suggests it has a strong connection to the gut as well.

Studies on the gut-brain axis reveal that dopamine production is influenced by gut health, meaning the physical state of the digestive system plays a role in the brain's reward system.[9] This means that our ability to feel motivated, whether to achieve a goal, stay disciplined, or follow through on commitments, can be directly affected by what's happening in our gut. Try tracking your energy and mood after different meals for a week to see how your gut affects motivation.

The gut signal impacts motivation in three primary ways:

- The gut signals energy availability: Motivation is naturally higher when our body is well-nourished and rested. Conversely, fatigue and nutrient depletion reduce dopamine levels, making tasks feel overwhelming.
- Emotional gut responses reinforce or deter actions: The "butterflies" we feel when excited and the "pit in our stomach" when dreading something are gut-based motivational signals. These physical sensations can either fuel or discourage action.
- The gut prioritizes survival over long-term planning: When under stress, the gut signal pushes for immediate relief over distant rewards, making it harder to stay motivated for goals that require patience and persistence.

Because of this, gut-dominant decision-makers often struggle with consistency. They may feel highly motivated one day but completely unmotivated the next, depending on external factors like sleep, stress, or food intake.

To strengthen motivation, the gut needs to be managed intentionally. This can include the following:

- optimizing gut health (through proper diet, hydration, and sleep)
- creating external accountability (to maintain motivation even when gut signals waver)
- recognizing when stress or fatigue is distorting motivation

In essence, the gut signal fuels motivation, influencing how much drive we feel toward a decision. While the heart may direct what we care about, and the mind may calculate how to achieve it, the gut often determines whether or not we take action. Eating too heavy of a lunch may make it difficult to return to work and tackle the project you left that morning.

The gut signal is often the most primal and immediate of the three signals. It's instinctual, reactive, and deeply tied to our biological and emotional needs. Unlike the head signal, which calculates and strategizes, or the heart signal, which connects and empathizes, the gut signal pulls us toward immediate action. It tells us when something is off before we can logically explain it. It makes us crave something before we fully understand why. It dictates our energy, drive, and decision-making ability in ways we often fail to notice until something feels off.

If you're a gut-dominant decision-maker, you likely have the following strengths:

- trust your instincts
- respond quickly to situations
- strong intuition

It's also highly likely that you have the following weaknesses:
- act impulsively
- demonstrate inconsistent reasoning
- have difficulty delaying gratification

The gut doesn't always ask permission before speaking. It doesn't wait for your head or your heart to weigh in. It just reacts. This reaction is sometimes with wisdom and sometimes with misplaced urgency.

Wise gut-dominant decision-makers know when to trust their gut and when to question it. They recognize that while the gut signal is powerful, it isn't always right. It needs balance. A gut instinct might warn you about a sketchy business deal, but it might also elicit panic when simply stepping outside your comfort zone. An urge might push you toward a bad habit or signal that something in your life needs attention. Motivation might surge one day and disappear the next, but that doesn't mean you've lost your passion. It just means your gut is affected by your environment, your energy, and your habits.

If the gut signal is a map, then you must learn to read it correctly. When you can do that, you gain the power to harness its wisdom rather than be ruled by its impulses. If nothing else, you gain the awareness to keep a snack on hand before making any major decisions.

SIGNAL COMPARISON CHART

	HEAD SIGNAL	HEART SIGNAL	GUT SIGNAL
PRIMARY VOICE	Logic & Analysis	Emotions & Connection	Instinct & Intuition
DEVELOPED THROUGH	Knowledge, observation, data	Relationships, emotions, inspiration	100+ million neurons in ENS
SOUNDS LIKE…	"What makes the most sense?"	"How do I feel about this?"	"What's my immediate reaction?"
SHOWS UP AS	• Reasoning & rationalization • Forecasting outcomes • Risk assessment • Pros & cons lists	• Feelings about situations • Emotional responses • Relational insights • What matters deeply	• Quick judgments • Physical sensations • Urges & cravings • Motivational levels
STRENGTH	Clarity, structure, objectivity	Passion, meaning, authenticity	Rapid responses, pattern recognition, survival instincts
GROWTH OPPORTUNITY	Analysis paralysis, overthinking	Emotional flooding, hurt-based hesitation	Impulsiveness, inconsistent reactions, need-based distortions
TRUST IT WHEN	You need facts & strategic planning	You need to honor what matters most	Immediate action needed or danger sensed
QUESTION IT WHEN	You're stuck in endless loops	Past pain is clouding judgment	You're hungry, tired, or stressed

PERSONAL REFLECTIONS – THE GUT SIGNAL

1. Considering my Decision Code quiz results, am I gut-dominant or not? If so, how do I identify with the Activator or Instinctive style?
2. How often do my urges drive my choices? Am I in control of them, or do they control me?
3. What are the most consistent motivations in my life? What keeps me moving forward?
4. Can I think of a time when my gut instinct saved me from a bad decision? What about a time when it misled me?

CHAPTER 4

WHERE DOES IT HURT?

"Traumatized people chronically feel unsafe inside their bodies."
—Bessel van der Kolk, MD

WHERE DOES IT HURT?

THE first time Malachi had food poisoning, he was staying at my parents' house. When we picked him up, he was lounging upside down on the couch, watching TV in that carefree, contorted way that only kids can. He seemed fine ... until he stood up.

"I don't feel good," he mumbled.

I asked the classic parent medical check question: "Where does it hurt?"

He responded sluggishly as he began rubbing his neck. "My neck hurts."

At first, we thought nothing of it. Maybe he'd tweaked something hanging upside down. But on the drive home, his complaints about his neck turned more persistent. Then, he became lethargic, which was so unlike him that alarm bells started going off in my mind. By the time we pulled into the driveway, he was miserable. Still clutching his neck, he collapsed onto the couch in clear distress.

I grabbed an ice pack, thinking maybe he'd strained something. But the moment I moved him to apply it, he threw up. Everywhere. All over our couch, our floor, just an absolute disaster. And, like most cases of food poisoning, he perked up immediately after purging.

"I guess it was my stomach, not my neck," he said, looking dazed but relieved.

That moment stuck with me not just because we needed a professional cleaner to salvage our couch but because it was such a perfect metaphor for something I see constantly as a counselor. Sometimes we don't know exactly where our pain is. We just know we *hurt*.

Malachi was in pain, but he couldn't pinpoint where that pain was coming from. His body knew something was wrong, but it sent confusing signals. As soon as the real source of pain was addressed, things improved. That's exactly how trauma works in our lives.

> Sometimes we don't know exactly where our pain is. We just know we hurt.

Sometimes we know we're hurting, but we can't quite figure out where that hurt is coming from. We might think we're facing a logical dilemma, an emotional struggle, or an instinctual warning, but what if that's not the case at all? **What if it's unprocessed trauma masquerading as a decision-making signal?**

WHAT TRAUMA IS (AND ISN'T)

Trauma is not just a bad memory or a difficult event; it is a wound that continues to affect how we think, feel, and make decisions. Peter Levine, a leader in trauma therapy, explains it this way: "Trauma isn't what happened to us; it's what happened inside us in the absence of an empathetic witness."[1] That last sentence is key. Trauma is more than just the severity of what we experience; it's about whether we have someone to help us process it. Many people assume they don't have trauma because they haven't faced extreme tragedy. However, unacknowledged pain, left without an empathetic witness, can still shape us in ways we don't realize.

When we hear the word *trauma*, most people think of life-altering events like abuse, violence, loss of a loved one, or catastrophic accidents. This is what we call big "T" trauma. These are the obvious, undeniable wounds that leave lasting marks. But there's another kind of trauma that's less visible but equally impactful: little "t" trauma. This kind of trauma comes from ongoing, subtle experiences that chip away at our sense of safety and self.

Maybe you grew up in a home where perfection was the standard and anything less brought disapproval. Or perhaps you experienced emotional neglect. This is not outright abuse but a consistent lack of validation and support. These experiences don't always scream *trauma*, but they can shape our worldview, influence our decisions, and create internal aches we don't fully understand.

Both kinds of trauma can distort the signals we rely on to make decisions. To break this down, I like to categorize trauma's impact on decision-making into three types of pain: headache, heartache, and stomachache. Each represents a different way that trauma can distort how we process choices.

Trauma is not about being weak, dramatic, or incapable. It's not something you can just "get over" by deciding to move on. Trauma is what happens when an experience overwhelms our ability to cope—when we carry pain that hasn't been fully processed. Until it is, that pain seeps into our decisions, often in ways that don't seem directly related.

Unresolved trauma can turn a clear head signal into a headache, a healthy heart signal into heartache, and a trustworthy gut signal into a stomachache. The key is learning to distinguish between a signal that's guiding you forward and an ache that's pulling you backward.

HEADACHE: WHEN PAIN DISRUPTS LOGIC AND REASON

An actual headache makes it hard to think. When your head is pounding, even simple decisions can feel overwhelming. You can't concentrate, you can't process things clearly, and you certainly can't think long term. When the pain of trauma impedes our logic and reasoning in decision-making, it's a very different but equally painful kind of headache.

People experiencing trauma-based cognitive impairment struggle with logic, planning, and rational thinking. Prolonged stress can shrink the PFC, the part responsible for decision-making, impulse control, and logical reasoning.[2] Instead of thinking critically, trauma survivors often become reactionary, making short-sighted or overly cautious decisions because their brains are prioritizing survival over strategy.

We all experience this to some degree. A stressful day at work can leave us feeling mentally exhausted, making even simple choices, like what to wear, seem impossible. On a larger scale, long-term trauma can cause chronic indecision, leading people to either shut down entirely or overcompensate by micromanaging every detail of their lives.

This kind of trauma-driven headache can be especially challenging for someone who is head-dominant in decision-making. These individuals typically rely on reason, planning, and structure to navigate life, so when trauma disrupts their ability to think clearly, they may spiral into overanalyzing or completely disengaging from decisions.

This isn't your head giving you a helpful signal. It's your unprocessed pain hijacking your logic. A head signal drives you forward with clarity and purpose. It helps you assess risks and make informed choices. A headache pulls you backward into doubt and fear. It keeps you stuck in endless loops of "what if" and "but maybe."

Let's say you're offered a promotion. A head signal would help you logically evaluate whether the new role aligns with your goals. A headache, however, might flood you with fears about failing, obsessing over every possible way it could go wrong, even if there's no real evidence to support those fears.

Healing here requires rebuilding trust in one's ability to reason without fear and recognizing that not every decision has to be a battle of risk assessment.

Additionally, healing often involves engaging in practices that help regulate cognitive overload. Techniques such as mindfulness and structured decision-making have been shown to help individuals rebuild the ability to process complex thoughts without succumbing to stress-induced paralysis. Sometimes, the most effective strategy is learning when to pause, breathe, and give the brain permission to rest.

HEARTACHE: WHEN PAIN DYSREGULATES EMOTIONS

Heartache doesn't just hurt; it distorts. When we are emotionally wounded, it becomes difficult to trust our feelings. One of the most well-documented effects of trauma is emotional dysregulation, which is the inability to manage emotions in a healthy way.[3] Trauma survivors often swing between emotional numbness and overwhelming intensity, making decision-making feel like navigating a storm without a compass.

We've all felt this, even in small ways. A difficult conversation can leave us emotionally raw, making us react more strongly than we normally would. When trauma runs deeper, it can cause people to either chase emotional highs, seeking validation through relationships, impulsive choices, and overcommitment, or shut down entirely, withdrawing from connection to avoid more pain.

For someone who is heart-dominant in decision-making, trauma-related heartache can lead to decisions that are purely driven by emotion, often at the expense of logic or gut instinct. You might feel overwhelmed by sadness, anger, or fear that doesn't quite match the situation at hand. Or you might shut down completely, avoiding decisions because the emotional weight feels too heavy. A heart signal brings warmth and connection. It helps you align your choices with your values and relationships. A heartache pulls you into emotional extremes. It makes you reactive, defensive, or disconnected.

Imagine you're deciding whether or not to reconcile with a friend after a falling out. A heart signal might guide you toward forgiveness if the relationship is valuable. A heartache, however, might flood you with unresolved pain from past betrayals, making it hard to see the situation clearly. Emotional reactions that do not fit the circumstance are a major symptom of heartache. As one of my favorite counselor sayings goes: "If it's hysterical, it's historical."

Healing in this space means learning to distinguish between your heart signal and your heartache and understanding that not every feeling needs to dictate an action.

Another essential component of healing from emotional dysregulation is learning how to tolerate discomfort without immediately reacting to it. Many trauma survivors make decisions in an attempt to escape pain rather than process it. Practicing emotional resilience through journaling, self-reflection, or therapy can help individuals build the ability to sit with their emotions rather than allowing them to dictate impulsive decisions.

STOMACHACHE: WHEN PAIN DISRUPTS JUDGMENT AND INSTINCTS

A stomachache throws everything off balance. It makes food seem untrustworthy, movement feel unnatural, and even the simplest decisions, like what to eat or how to sit, suddenly become sources of discomfort. Trauma has a similar effect on our judgment and instincts, causing us to second-guess what should come naturally.

Studies have shown that trauma can heighten the amygdala's response to perceived threats, leading individuals to see danger where there is none.[4] This overactive survival mechanism can make people hypervigilant, avoidant, or impulsive, constantly switching between extreme caution and reckless decision-making in an attempt to regain control.

On a small scale, this might look like struggling with indecisiveness, feeling paralyzed over small choices, or doubting one's gut feelings in everyday situations. On a larger scale, trauma-related pain in our gut can lead to chronic mistrust of one's own instincts, resulting in patterns of avoidance, self-sabotage, or impulsivity.

For someone who is gut-dominant in decision-making, this kind of trauma can be particularly unsettling. These individuals typically rely on their instincts to guide them, but when trauma distorts that inner compass, they may feel completely disconnected from themselves.

You might feel a constant sense of dread, even when there's no real threat, or you might impulsively make choices to get rid of the discomfort. A gut signal is quick and confident. It gives you a sense of "this feels right" or "this feels off" without overanalyzing. A stomachache is persistent and nagging. It's driven by fear and often feels like a physical burden of tightness in your chest, a pit in your stomach, or a sense of restlessness.

Imagine you're thinking about starting a new project. A gut signal might give you an immediate sense of excitement or hesitation based on your instincts. A stomachache, however, might make you feel paralyzed with fear about failing, even if you have all the skills and support you need. Healing in this area often involves rebuilding trust in one's ability to sense, interpret, and act on gut feelings without fear.

The Decision Code teaches us to listen to our head, heart, and gut signals when making choices. But trauma complicates that process. It creates noise that can drown out true signals, making it hard to know what's guiding us. Here's the key: Signals drive us forward; aches pull us backward. A signal is about what's happening *right now*. It's grounded in the present and aligned with your current values and goals. An ache is about something that's already happened. It's rooted in past pain and unprocessed emotions.

When you're unsure if you're feeling a signal or an ache, ask yourself the following questions:

- Is this reaction about the present situation, or is it tied to something from my past?
- Am I moving forward with clarity, or am I being pulled backward by fear or pain?

When your response feels disproportionate to the situation, it's often a sign that old wounds are influencing your decision-making.

DISTINGUISHING TRUE GUIDANCE FROM TRAUMA RESPONSES

ASPECT	TRUE SIGNAL	TRAUMA ACHE
DIRECTION	Drives you forward	Pulls you backward
TIME FOCUS	Present moment	Past pain/future fears
FEELING	Clear, aligned	Disproportionate, stuck
PHYSICAL	Focused sensation	Persistent discomfort
RESULT	Progress & clarity	Avoidance & confusion
EXAMPLE	"This feels right for now."	"What if I get hurt again?"

HEALING THE ACHES TO HEAR THE SIGNALS

Trauma doesn't have to define your decisions. Below are five steps to recognize and heal your aches so you can clear the noise and reconnect with your true signals:

1. **Acknowledge the ache:** Recognize when trauma is influencing your decisions and name it. "I'm feeling overwhelmed because this situation reminds me of past hurt."
2. **Process the pain:** Whether through therapy, journaling, or talking with a trusted friend, give yourself space to process the emotions tied to your trauma. This helps you separate past pain from present decisions.
3. **Practice self-compassion:** Be gentle with yourself as you navigate this process. Healing takes time, and it's okay to make mistakes along the way.
4. **Use The Decision Code:** As you heal, return to The Decision Code. Check in with your head, heart, and gut. Are your signals aligned? If not, explore what's holding you back.
5. **Stay present:** When making decisions, focus on the present moment. Ask yourself, *What do I need right now?* This helps you stay grounded in reality rather than being pulled into past pain.

Trauma complicates decision-making, but it doesn't have to control it. By learning to distinguish between your true signals and the aches of unprocessed pain, you can make choices that align with your values, goals, and authentic self.

The journey of healing isn't about eliminating all pain. It's about recognizing when that pain is influencing your decisions and gently guiding yourself back to clarity. When your head, heart, and gut are aligned, you'll live in ways that feel true to who you are.

Like Malachi clutching his neck when the real issue was his stomach, trauma can make us misidentify the source of our pain. We think we just have a headache and try to think our way out of it. We think we just have a heartache, so we chase emotional highs. We think we just have a stomachache, so we shut down our instincts. But the real issue is often deeper, rooted in unresolved pain that needs to be addressed.

The best decisions come from understanding pain, not ignoring it. When we recognize *where* trauma is affecting us, we can begin making choices that lead toward healing rather than further harm.

PERSONAL REFLECTIONS – WHERE DOES IT HURT?

1. Do I tend to misidentify my pain? Do I assume my struggle is in one area when it's actually rooted somewhere deeper?
2. Which type of trauma-related ache—headache, heartache, or stomachache—do I most resonate with in my decision-making patterns?
3. If I am head-dominant, heart-dominant, or gut-dominant in my decision-making, how does that shape the way I process pain?
4. Have I had an empathetic witness in my life to help me process difficult moments, or have I had to carry them alone?
5. What is one step I can take to better understand and process my pain so that it doesn't dictate my decisions?

CHAPTER 5

KNOWING GOD

"You will seek me and find me when you seek me with all your heart."
—Jeremiah 29:13 (NIV)

I'M a church kid through and through. I have many unique junctures in my story where my faith became more personal, but the backdrop of my belief system was instilled in me at home and in my environment. Being a church kid certainly has its quirks. I'm still not totally sure why *The Smurfs* and *Rugrats* were banned in my home, but they definitely were. My earliest ideas of God were born from object lessons in children's church, Bible stories read by puppets, and parables illustrated on my coloring page. Those little pages were my stained glass windows and, in the same way, helped me *see* God. Eventually, however, my experience of God had to grow beyond something engaged around me to something encountered deep within me. I believe God shows up in all three of our signals.

If faith is a journey, then experiencing God is not a single road. Some encounter Him first through intellect, others through emotion, and others through the undeniable pull of His direction in their lives. However we come to know Him, the reality of His presence touches all three parts of our being: our head (logic and understanding), our heart (deep emotion and

> If faith is a journey, then experiencing God is not a single road. Some encounter Him first through intellect, others through emotion, and others through the undeniable pull of His direction in their lives.

presence), and our gut (instinct and direction).

If you are reading this and faith is not something that resonates with you, I want to give you space to continue this book without feeling like you have to force yourself into something that doesn't align with your beliefs. Part Two of this book will continue exploring the ways we make decisions, and I welcome you to engage with the material in whatever way is meaningful to you. But for those who are curious about what it means to know God in the fullness of our being, this chapter is for you. We'll explore how we encounter God in our head, heart, and gut, and examine three women from Scripture who particularly capture the essence of them.

GOD IN THE HEAD: THE GOD OF LOGIC AND UNDERSTANDING

For many, the journey of faith begins in the mind. The Bible invites us to reason, seek wisdom, and engage intellectually with who God is. Proverbs 2:6 tells us,
"For the Lord gives wisdom; from His mouth come knowledge and understanding" (NIV). Faith is not a blind leap but a deeply considered conviction built on truth.

No biblical figure illustrates this pursuit of wisdom quite like the Queen of Sheba. She's a fascinating figure who bursts into the Old Testament narrative almost unannounced. She had heard of King Solomon's legendary wisdom but wasn't content with hearsay. She traveled a great distance to test him with difficult questions, seeking firsthand knowledge and proof of his understanding (1 Kings 10:1–9). When she saw the depth of his wisdom and the way it aligned with God's truth, she didn't just admire Solomon; she recognized that his wisdom came from the Lord. Her encounter with God in her head allowed her to know Him personally.

Like the Queen of Sheba, those who encounter God through study and inquiry are not satisfied with surface-level faith. They ask hard questions, seek evidence, and examine Scripture to develop a deeper understanding. Their faith is strengthened not by ignoring doubts but by wrestling through them. But knowledge alone is not enough. A relationship with God cannot be contained to facts and doctrine. It must move from the head to the heart.

Those who primarily know God through study may sometimes struggle with feeling disconnected from His presence. They might find themselves relying on theology without intimacy, thinking they can reason their way into faith. But God does not simply want to be understood; He wants to be known. Faith in its fullness is not just about knowledge but about relationship.

When we find ourselves in a headache, and doubt, confusion, or over-intellectualization clouds our faith, God is there. He restores clarity, reminding us that truth is not just an idea but a person, Jesus Christ. He invites us not only to learn about Him but to trust Him, even in the gaps of our understanding.

GOD IN THE HEART: THE GOD OF PRESENCE AND EMOTION

If the mind seeks to understand God, the heart longs to feel Him. There is a reason that Scripture tells us to "love the Lord your God with all your heart" (Deuteronomy 6:5). Faith is more than intellectual assent. It is about encountering the presence of God in a way that transforms our emotions and affections.

The woman who washed Jesus' feet exemplifies this kind of faith (Luke 7:36–50). She wasn't concerned with theological debates or proving anything to anyone. She didn't even need to ask a question. She was overwhelmed with love and gratitude, so much so that she fell at Jesus' feet, weeping as she anointed Him with oil. Her faith was deeply felt, not just known. She didn't need an argument for why Jesus was worthy because she experienced His presence and responded with everything she had.

For those who are heart-dominant in their faith, these experiences are essential. They connect with God through worship, through relationships, and through the beauty of creation. They feel His presence in prayer and moments of deep emotion. But just as knowledge without emotion can be cold, emotion without understanding can be unstable. Faith must be both felt and grounded.

When we experience heartache, and loss, grief, or loneliness overwhelm us, God is there. He doesn't just offer comfort from a distance; He enters into our sorrow, weeping with us and holding us in our brokenness. He is the God who is near to the brokenhearted (Psalm 34:18), bringing healing through His love.

GOD IN THE GUT: THE GOD OF GUIDANCE AND DIRECTION

There are times when God speaks not in words but in urgency. Times when you feel a stirring so deep in your being that you know you must move, act, or trust even when the path ahead is uncertain. This is the experience of God in the gut, where He directs, convicts, and compels.

Elizabeth, the mother of John the Baptist, experienced this in a profound way (Luke 1:41–45). When Mary, pregnant with Jesus, entered her home, Elizabeth didn't need an explanation. She felt it. Scripture tells us that the baby in her womb leaped for joy, and in that moment, she knew. Before Mary even spoke, Elizabeth recognized the presence of the Messiah.

For those who are gut-dominant in their faith, obedience is their greatest act of trust. They move forward because they feel God's prompting. But discernment is key, and learning to recognize the difference between God's leading and mere impulse requires wisdom and faith.

When we experience a stomachache, and fear, anxiety, or uncertainty paralyzes us, God is there. He strengthens our steps, reminding us that He goes before us (Deuteronomy 31:8) and that we can trust Him even when we can't see the whole path ahead.

To know God fully is to experience Him through understanding, presence, and guidance. The Queen of Sheba sought God through wisdom and inquiry. The woman who washed Jesus' feet found Him through love and presence. Elizabeth encountered Him through discernment and action.

Each of these women knew God differently, yet all were profoundly changed by their encounters with Him.

God meets us in all three areas. He speaks to our minds, giving us wisdom when we seek understanding. He reaches our hearts, offering deep connection and love. He resonates deeply, even in our gut, guiding us when we need direction. He also heals the aches in all three places by lifting confusion, soothing brokenness, and steadying uncertainty.

Faith rarely provides all the answers. Instead, it is about walking in relationship with a God who is both knowable and beyond comprehension. In that journey, we come to see that knowing God is not just about grasping an idea but rather about being known by Him.

GOD USES ALL THREE SIGNALS

God doesn't just speak in one way; He reaches us through all three signals. Sometimes He speaks through wisdom and understanding, guiding us with logic and Scripture. Other times, He meets us in emotion, overwhelming us with His presence and love. And other times, He moves us through deep, internal conviction, nudging us toward action.

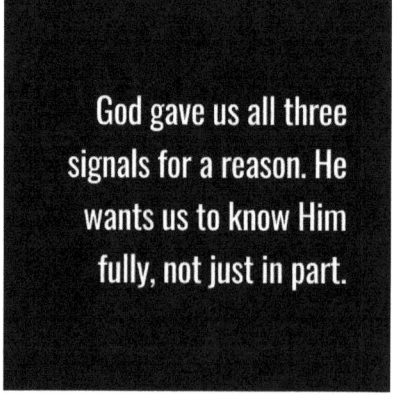

God gave us all three signals for a reason. He wants us to know Him fully, not just in part.

Like in decision-making, the strongest faith comes when all three signals align. When our head understands, our heart feels, and our gut trusts, we experience a deep and complete relationship with God. But often, one area is stronger than the others, and that's where we should lean in to grow.

Consider implementing the following strategies:

- If you mostly engage God with your mind, challenge yourself to open your heart more in worship and trust. Explore moments of silence and reflection beyond study.
- If you mostly feel God through emotion, seek deeper understanding in Scripture and theology. Anchor your faith in truth, not just experience.
- If you mostly sense God through instinct, test what you feel against Scripture and wise counsel. Develop the discipline to confirm your inner knowing.

God gave us all three signals for a reason. He wants us to know Him fully, not just in part. Learning to experience Him in all three ways unlocks a richer, more balanced faith. The Decision Code helps us make everyday choices, and it also helps us understand how we relate to the biggest decision of all: how we know God.

PERSONAL REFLECTIONS – KNOWING GOD

1. Do I most often experience God through my head, heart, or gut?
2. Have I ever neglected one way of knowing God while relying too much on another?
3. Where do I need healing in my faith? Do I struggle with doubt, emotional disconnection, or fear of making the wrong decisions?
4. How has God led me in the past through wisdom, presence, or direction?
5. What is one way I can seek to experience God in a new way this week?

PART TWO

YES, BUT...

"You don't have to see the whole staircase, just take the first step."
—Martin Luther King Jr.

MAKING decisions isn't always about complete certainty. Sometimes, two signals give you a clear yes, but one signal holds you back. This part of the book explores how to move forward wisely when faced with internal hesitation. However, there's another layer we need to explore. When one signal is ignored for too long, it can hijack the other signals, distorting the decision-making process altogether.

THE HIJACKING EFFECT: WHEN AN IGNORED SIGNAL MASQUERADES AS ANOTHER

One of my most significant battles in life was with anxiety. I'll discuss this more later, but for years, I ignored the emotional pain that my heart signal was desperately trying to make me acknowledge. My heart was telling me to stop, process, and feel, but I kept pushing it down, thinking I could just keep moving forward. But the heart signal, refusing to be ignored, hijacked my head and gut, making it seem as if the problem was something else entirely. Anxiety took over my head, creating racing thoughts, obsessive overanalysis, and worst-case-scenario thinking. It took over my gut, creating a constant churn, nausea, and an overwhelming sense of dread. But it wasn't actually a head issue or a gut issue. It was my heart demanding attention, disguising itself as a logical crisis and a physical warning.

When one signal is chronically ignored, it doesn't just stay silent. It expands itself, hijacking the others until it's finally acknowledged. This leads to confusion in decision-making because what you think is a head signal might be unresolved emotional pain from the heart. What you believe is a gut instinct might be your head trying to maintain control over fear.

> When one signal is chronically ignored, it doesn't just stay silent. It expands itself, hijacking the others until it's finally acknowledged.

WHEN THE UNPROCESSED HEART SIGNAL HIJACKS THE HEAD

A strong head signal should bring clarity, structure, and reason. However, when the heart hijacks the head, it disguises emotional pain as logic. Instead of recognizing deep-seated emotional wounds, a person may experience their distress as overanalyzing, perfectionism, or an obsessive need for control.

Instead of acknowledging emotional pain, someone might endlessly strategize, analyze, or research, believing they are being logical when they are actually avoiding feelings. This feels like racing thoughts, decision paralysis, an overwhelming need for certainty, or difficulty trusting others.

Say a person who has been deeply hurt in past relationships is now struggling to connect. They might convince themselves they "just haven't found the right person" rather than acknowledging their heart is afraid of vulnerability. They frame their hesitancy as logical skepticism when, in reality, it is unresolved heartbreak.

To recognize if your heart has hijacked your head, ask yourself the following questions:

- Is this truly logic speaking, or am I just avoiding emotional discomfort?
- Would I still feel this hesitancy if I had no history of pain in this area?

WHEN AN OVERACTIVE HEAD SIGNAL HIJACKS THE GUT

A true gut signal is instinctual, quick, decisive, and clear. But when an overactive head hijacks the gut, it creates a sense of false intuition that is merely fear disguised as instinct. Instead of a deep, confident knowing, it feels more like hypervigilance and constant second-guessing.

A person may believe they have a "bad feeling" about something when, in reality, they are just mentally overloaded with analysis and risk calculations. This produces a persistent sense of unease, tension in the body, an inability to rest, and a tendency to interpret everything as a warning sign.

Consider someone facing a career change who might feel an overwhelming sense of dread that convinces them, *This must be a bad idea.* That's not their gut talking; it's their head flooding their system with every possible failure scenario, making them mistake anxiety for intuition.

To explore this, ask yourself the following questions:

- Is my gut instinct coming from a place of deep knowing, or is it just my head overwhelming me with fear?
- If I weren't overthinking this, would my gut feel differently?

WHEN A SUPPRESSED GUT SIGNAL HIJACKS THE HEART

The heart brings passion, connection, and deep emotional experiences. But when an ignored gut signal hijacks the heart, emotions become exaggerated or misdirected. Instead of feeling emotions for what they truly are, a person may project their unacknowledged fears or instincts onto situations and people.

A person may feel extreme attachment, urgency, or emotional distress that seems disproportionate to the situation. This produces overwhelming longing, desperate emotions, an inability to let go, or a tendency to rationalize unhealthy relationships or decisions.

Someone in a toxic relationship may feel like they "just can't let go" because they are so emotionally invested. But deep down, their gut has been warning them all along that the other person is unhealthy for them. Instead of listening to the gut's quiet voice, the ignored gut signal fuels extreme heart-driven emotions, making them believe they are "meant" to stay.

To better understand, reflect on the following questions:
- Are my emotions aligned with reality, or is my heart carrying the weight of an ignored instinct?

- If I truly trusted my intuition, would I still feel this strongly?

RECOGNIZING WHEN A SIGNAL IS BEING HIJACKED

A true signal moves you forward. A hijacked signal keeps you stuck.

To determine whether what you're experiencing is a genuine signal or a disguised ache, ask yourself the following questions:
- Am I resisting or ignoring something deeper? If so, which signal am I ignoring?
- Is this feeling rooted in the present, or is it tied to past pain or future fears? A true signal is about the present moment, while a hijacked signal often comes from unresolved wounds.
- Does this decision feel freeing, or does it feel like a desperate attempt to fix or control something? True signals bring clarity. Hijacked signals create urgency, doubt, or avoidance.

Recognizing when an ignored signal is hijacking the others can bring clarity back into your decision-making process. The goal isn't to let any one signal dominate but to integrate all three—head, heart, and gut—to inform your decisions.

Let's imagine you truly understand how to access your head, heart, and gut signals. You know the difference between a signal and an ache and recognize where some internal hijacking has happened. You're ready to use The Decision Code, but the inevitable happens. You're trying to make a decision, but two signals say yes, and one says no. You're stuck in an internal conflict, wondering what to decide.

I recall the moment my wife and I had to decide whether or not to launch our company. My life was already full, and I was juggling responsibilities, time commitments, and relationships that meant a lot to me. Saying yes to something new felt like it would disrupt everything. My head knew it was a necessary step. My heart felt deeply called to it. But my gut? My gut was terrified.

What if I disappointed people by shifting my focus? What if I couldn't handle the pressure? What if I failed?

That's the reality of decision-making. Some choices are easy when all three inner signals are in perfect harmony. Your head (logic), heart (emotion), and gut (instinct) are all saying the same thing, and you can move forward with clarity. But most big decisions aren't like that. Most of the time, people get stuck because these three signals are in conflict.

Indecisiveness isn't about lacking intelligence or confidence; it's about internal misalignment. Psychological research backs this up. Studies on decision paralysis show that when people experience conflicting motivations, their brains struggle to process a clear path forward.[5] Cognitive dissonance theory suggests that we experience stress when our beliefs, emotions, or instincts contradict each other. In other words, the turmoil we feel in decision-making isn't random; it's our mind, heart, and gut fighting for control.[6]

If these three signals shape our understanding of the world, it makes sense that they also shape how we make decisions. The challenge comes when they don't agree. Through years of coaching and counseling, I've seen that most people don't struggle with decision-making because they don't know what to do. They struggle because they feel torn between what they think is right (head), what they feel is right (heart), and what they sense is right (gut). When those three areas aren't speaking the same language, we hesitate. We second-guess. We get stuck.

But here's the good news: Decision-making doesn't have to feel like a battleground. There's a way to navigate the tension with confidence.

THE CONSEQUENCES OF INDECISION

Indecision slows us down and shapes the way we see ourselves. When we delay making choices, we send an internal message that we don't trust our own judgment. Over time, this erodes our confidence and makes every future decision feel heavier. Hesitation trains us to expect failure before we've even taken a step.

Not only that, but indecision can place a burden on the people around us. Whether it's in leadership, relationships, or family life, people depend on us to make choices. When we hesitate too long, it forces others to wait in uncertainty or make the decision for us. And while they might not say it outright, others lose confidence in us when they sense we don't have confidence in ourselves.

In counseling, I've seen indecision become a form of avoidance. When someone fears making the wrong choice, they sometimes think delaying the decision will make things easier. But the reality is that time doesn't always bring clarity. It often just brings more anxiety. The longer we sit in uncertainty, the more pressure builds, making the decision feel even riskier than it was before.

This is why learning to navigate internal conflict is so critical. Instead of letting fear of mistakes keep us stuck, we need a process for moving forward with confidence even when we don't have perfect clarity.

HOW TO MAKE DECISIONS WITH CONFIDENCE

This section of the book explores what to do when one part of you is holding back.

Here's the simplest way to understand The Decision Code:

- If two of your decision signals are saying yes but one is hesitant, move forward, but give attention to what's holding you back.
- If two of your decision signals are saying no, but one is pushing forward, say no because that compulsion is usually not wisdom.

When your head is holding you back, you're overthinking. When your heart is holding you back, you're hurt. When your gut is holding you back, you're afraid.

Each of these creates its own unique struggle, and each requires a different approach to move forward.

This framework is more than a theory; it's something I've seen play out repeatedly in coaching and counseling. I've worked with clients who were stuck in jobs they hated because their heart told them to stay loyal, even when their head and gut screamed, *Get out!* I've seen people stay in unhealthy relationships because their gut was deeply attached, even though their head and heart were warning them otherwise. I've seen people pass up life-changing opportunities because their gut was afraid to take the leap, even when their head and heart knew it was the right move.

One of the most frustrating things about decision-making is that we often assume the best choices should feel easy, but that's rarely the case. Growth and progress almost always come with some level of discomfort. Sometimes we mistake a necessary challenge for a sign that we're making the wrong decision, but discomfort isn't always a warning. Sometimes, it's part of the process.

We make stronger choices when we learn to listen to these signals with discernment. Instead of waiting for perfect clarity, we can move forward with confidence, knowing that clarity often comes in motion, not before it.

THE COURAGE TO DECIDE

There's a reason most people avoid making decisions: Choosing one path means closing the door on others. Every decision involves loss. Even when choosing something good, we're always leaving something else behind. That's why so many people get stuck in decision-making. It's not because they don't know the right answer. They don't want to deal with the weight of closing the other doors.

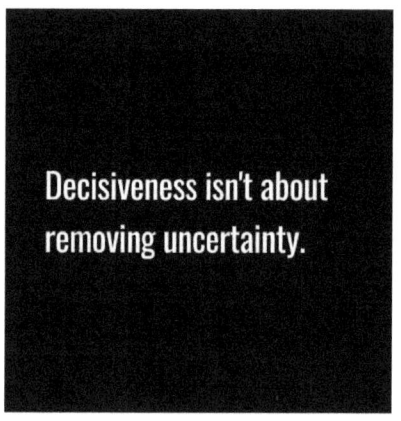

But avoiding decisions doesn't remove the pain of loss; it just spreads it out over time. When we refuse to make a decision, we're still making one. We're choosing to stay in uncertainty rather than step into a new reality.

Over the next three chapters, I'll unpack how overthinking (head), hurt (heart), and fear (gut) create resistance in decision-making. I'll share real client stories, personal experiences, and practical tools for overcoming these blocks.

Decisiveness isn't about removing uncertainty. It's about learning to trust your head, heart, and gut without waiting for them to agree perfectly. It's about making wise, balanced choices even when one part of you is hesitant. And it's about knowing that you can move forward even when the answer is: Yes, but …

CHAPTER 6

WHEN YOUR HEAD HOLDS YOU BACK (OVERTHINKING)

"Nothing in life is to be feared; it is only to be understood."
—Marie Curie

WHEN YOUR HEAD HOLDS YOU BACK (OVERTHINKING)

AS a senior in high school on a mission trip to Honduras, I stood at the edge of a twenty-five-foot cliff, looking down at the river below. The pristine flow of the river was beautiful, but the crashing waterfall to my left was even more stunning. The rock I'd climbed to was a popular spot from which to jump into the river far below. I had seen others do it. My friends were in the water cheering me on. I wanted the thrill of the jump. But my head? My head had other plans.

I could feel my brain going into overdrive. It calculated the height. It ran the numbers on how fast I'd hit the water. It imagined scenarios like twisting an ankle, landing wrong, some unknown danger lurking beneath the surface, or my shorts flying off—a real terror. The more I thought, the more impossible the jump felt. My thoughts were feeding themselves, making the cliff seem higher, the water darker, the risk greater.

To make matters worse, my friends had started a countdown. They chanted, "Three, two, ONE!" thinking it would help. I thought it would help, too. I was sure that I was sending my body forward over the edge, but somehow, when the countdown ended, my legs jumped back, not forward. The racing thoughts in my head muffled their chanting. Eventually, I had a choice: keep thinking or just jump. So I jumped. Well, first I made a rather embarrassing grunt and whimper as I launched myself over the edge, but then I jumped. The rush was incredible. The water was perfect. My shorts were still on. As I surfaced, gasping with exhilaration, the first thought that hit me was, *Why did I wait so long?* The answer had nothing to do with the cliff but everything to do with my head. Overthinking is a common experience for all of us.

THE PROBLEM: THE OVERACTIVE HEAD SIGNAL

The head signal is essential. It helps us reason, analyze, and forecast outcomes. But when the head signal becomes overactive, it shifts us out of logic and into overthinking. Instead of guiding us wisely, it paralyzes us with worst-case scenario forecasting and perfectionism.

Overthinking makes us question every move: *What if I fail? What if I regret it? What if I look foolish?* These thoughts can delay decisions and often keep us from making them at all.

Worse, overthinking often disguises itself as wisdom. Many people don't realize they're stuck in their heads because they call it "being rational" or "just making sure." They convince themselves that gathering more information is the smart move when, in reality, they're avoiding the discomfort of making a decision and moving forward.

This doesn't just affect major life choices. Overthinking happens daily. Maybe you hesitate to send that email, apply for the promotion, have the difficult conversation, or say yes to an opportunity that excites you but also scares you. The head signal, when mismanaged, keeps you stuck in a cycle of questioning rather than acting.

THE SCIENCE OF OVERTHINKING DECISIONS

Overthinking isn't just a bad habit; it's a neurological loop that can weaken our ability to make sound decisions. The brain's prefrontal cortex, responsible for reasoning, can become overloaded when analyzing too many variables. Instead of clarity, we experience decision fatigue, making it harder to act.

Excessive analysis weakens logical reasoning abilities, making people more likely to avoid decisions altogether. The brain treats every scenario as a new risk, reinforcing avoidance rather than action.

One study revealed that people who overanalyze their decisions are often less satisfied with their choices than those who decide quickly.[1] The longer we analyze, the more uncertain we become, leading to poor choices or no choice at all.

WHEN THE HEART AND GUT SAY YES, BUT THE HEAD SAYS NO

This is where the conflict truly begins. Imagine feeling a deep pull in your gut telling you to move forward, whether that's taking a leap in your career, starting a new relationship, or making a bold life change. Your heart is all in, feeling the excitement, the passion, the emotional certainty that this is the right thing to do. And yet, your head refuses to get on board.

Physically, this kind of inner conflict can feel like the following:

- tension in the shoulders and neck, like a literal weight of decision-making
- headaches from thinking in circles
- restlessness or lying awake at night, running through the same arguments again and again

Mentally, this inner conflict shows up as the following:

- over-researching: reading every article, listening to every opinion, but never feeling ready
- playing out worst-case scenarios: convincing yourself that any move forward could end in disaster
- seeking endless validation: asking ten people for advice but ignoring your gut feeling
- perfectionism: believing you need absolute certainty before making a move

This kind of overthinking keeps us trapped in indecision, preventing us from embracing the opportunities our heart and gut already know we should take. As you become more in tune with the three signals of decision-making, you'll notice when you're encountering a conflict coming from the head signal because it almost presents itself as overthinking.

MICHAEL AND THE WEIGHT OF OVERTHINKING

Michael, a client of mine, was stuck in his head about whether and how he could proceed with the business he'd built. He had devoted years to his organization but was now questioning everything. He felt jaded, cynical, and unsure. Every decision led to more questions: *Is this worth it? Am I wasting my time? Will this even succeed? What else could I do?*

On paper, his questions seemed practical, as he analyzed risks and weighed options. The more he unpacked his thoughts, though, it became clear: His hesitation wasn't rooted in facts or careful consideration; it was rooted in scarcity and frustration, which led to an endless loop of questions.

I asked Michael how he got to this point and what it would take to get out, and he acknowledged his pattern was familiar. He had once been blindly optimistic, assuming everything would work out as he hoped. When things didn't go as planned, he overcorrected, moving from unquestioned confidence to constant doubt. Now, instead of moving forward, he was paralyzed with conflict, asking endless questions to cope with the sinking feeling that he'd wasted years of effort. A conflict stemming from the head signal like this results in a desperate attempt to figure things out and find certainty that cannot actually be found.

Michael's breakthrough came when he realized that his hesitation and attitude were costing him more than failure ever could. The time, energy, and momentum he was losing in this very understandable spiral were greater risks than he realized. Once he shifted his mindset, he engaged with action again, and things started falling into place. His heart and gut were sure he needed to continue on his path, but his head had been overthinking what that meant. He resolved to continue doing what he'd always done, but *differently*. He committed to ensuring his time and effort weren't in overdrive so he could tend to the questions of worth and value. Time spent with loved ones or resting was just as important as time spent working hard.

Michael's story is not unique. Overthinking masquerades as logic in many of our lives. I've heard many people doubt or question their circumstances. It convinces us that we need more time, information, or certainty before we can continue. But in reality, no amount of preparation will eliminate the unknowns completely. The only way to move past uncertainty is to act in the face of it.

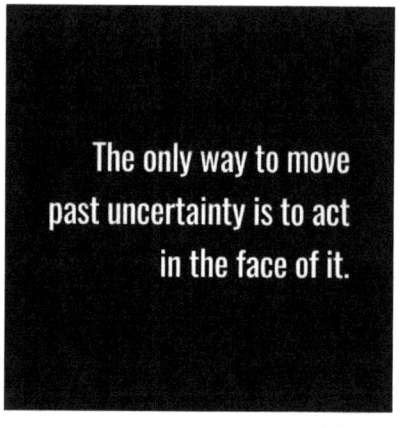

Biblically, we see that overthinking isn't wisdom. James 1:5–6, reminds us: "If any of you lacks wisdom, let him ask God, who gives generously to all without reproach, and it will be given to him. But let him ask in faith, with no doubting, for the one who doubts is like a wave of the sea that is driven and tossed by the wind" (ESV).

Doubt and overthinking make us unstable. Scripture continually shows that faith requires movement. If we wait for perfect clarity before making decisions, we'll never take the first step.

TOOLS TO OVERCOME OVERTHINKING

1. **Talk it out:** Overthinking thrives in isolation. Discussing decisions with mentors, coaches, or trusted friends can help break the cycle of analysis paralysis.
2. **Journal to slow overthinking:** Writing out your thoughts helps you identify patterns and see where your head is getting stuck in unnecessary loops.
3. **The overthinking filter framework:** Before delaying a decision, ask yourself,
   o   Am I waiting for certainty, or do I already know what I should do?
   o   What would I do if I weren't overthinking?
   o   Is more information helping me or just keeping me stuck?
4. **Take small actions:** Clarity comes from doing, not thinking. Start small, but start. Movement is the only true antidote to overthinking.
5. **Set a decision deadline:** Give yourself a timeframe to analyze, but then decide and move forward.

The head signal is powerful, but it must be managed. Overthinking will never lead to clarity; it only leads to hesitation. Wisdom considers the facts, but wisdom also moves.

So when your head starts replaying scenarios, craving more certainty, and calling overanalysis "logic," step back and ask: *Is my hesitation really wisdom, or am I just stuck in my head?* The moment you see it for what it is, you can silence the noise, take a deep breath, and leap.

Overthinking will always try to keep you at the edge of the cliff. But if you want to experience the thrill of the jump and the freedom, the growth, the success it brings, you have to choose to leap anyway.

PERSONAL REFLECTIONS - WHEN YOUR HEAD HOLDS YOU BACK (OVERTHINKING)

1. What's a decision in my life where fear has held me back?
2. Where do I disguise fear as wisdom?
3. How does my head signal usually react to fear?
    - Do I get stuck in analysis?
    - Do I seek external validation, hoping someone else will make the choice for me?
4. What is a fear-driven decision I regret?
5. What's one small action I can take toward something I've been avoiding?
6. If I wasn't afraid, what decision would I make today?

CHAPTER 7

WHEN YOUR HEART HOLDS YOU BACK (HURT)

"Grief is the price we pay for love."
—Queen Elizabeth II

WHEN YOUR HEART HOLDS YOU BACK (HURT)

IT still hurts to talk about it. Death is never easy, but the death of a young man in the prime of his life is an unusually painful injustice and grief. This young man was my best friend, Dave. Dave and I were the two youngest pastors at our church, so naturally we spent the most time together. I think we were together every day, either in the office or at his apartment, playing video games. He was a gentle, quirky dude who somehow put up with my not-so-gentle quirks.

His battle with cancer was the kind of pain that shakes the foundation of who you are. What was supposed to be a six-month prognosis became a valiant two-year battle. If you've loved someone during their cancer journey, you understand how grueling it is. The prayers that I and many others prayed for his healing were so fervent, but watching him deteriorate was heartbreaking. His passing hurt so deeply that I didn't know what to do with it. Being head-dominant, I defaulted into "fix it" mode. I tried to take care of his wife and daughter, stepped in to care for the youth group he pastored, and ensured others were processing their grief. But I refused to process my

> **Anxiety is like a fire alarm in your body alerting you to something unattended in your heart.**

own. My heart was signaling pain, and I ignored it, pushing forward with logic, productivity, and problem-solving. I convinced myself that if I just kept moving, I wouldn't have to feel it.

But pain doesn't just disappear because we avoid it. Over the next decade, the unprocessed grief reached its breaking point. My body started responding with symptoms of panic disorder. I couldn't breathe. I couldn't sleep. I couldn't get close to people because the possibility of more hurt felt unbearable. Anxiety is like a fire alarm in your body alerting you to something unattended to in your heart. My heart had been trying to send me a message, and I had silenced it for too long. It wasn't until I acknowledged the hurt and processed it in ways I'd always avoided that I was able to heal and move forward.

I'll take this opportunity to mention that if you relate at all to some of my story, and have faced a tragic loss of a person, or another type of loss in your life, my wife, Amanda McNeil's book *Overcoming the Overcast: Navigating the Storms of Grief with God* is the kind of resource I wish I had when I went through my tragedy. I believe it will bless you.

THE PROBLEM: EMOTIONAL PAIN AS AN OVERACTIVE HEART SIGNAL

While my story has some unique pain to it, all of us carry pain in some way. The heart signal is powerful. It helps us connect, feel deeply, and engage in relationships with passion and vulnerability.

But when the heart is wounded, it struggles to function properly. Instead of guiding us toward healthy connection, it either shuts down entirely or floods us with overwhelming emotion.

When the heart is holding someone back, it usually shows up in one of two ways: emotional flooding or emotional shutdown. Emotional flooding feels like an overwhelming tidal wave of grief, anger, sadness, or anxiety crashing down all at once. It makes decision-making feel impossible because the pain is too intense to think clearly. On the other hand, emotional shutdown is a numbing response. It's when past hurt has made us so afraid of feeling again that we build walls around our hearts, refusing to engage deeply in anything that might expose us to more pain.

Unresolved pain leads to questioning others (Can I trust them?) or questioning ourselves (Can I handle this?). It distorts reality, making us hesitant to take risks, trust people, or embrace new opportunities. Worse, people often justify staying stuck in their pain. They tell themselves they *can't* move forward, that it's just how they are, or that others are responsible for their hurt. But the truth is, avoiding pain doesn't heal it.

THE SCIENCE OF EMOTIONAL PAIN AND DECISION PARALYSIS

Emotional pain is not just an abstract feeling. It is processed in the brain similarly to physical pain. The brain's anterior cingulate cortex, which processes physical pain, is also activated during emotional distress. This explains why heartbreak, grief, and betrayal *physically hurt*.

Unresolved emotional pain impacts cognitive function. People experiencing prolonged grief, trauma, or relational wounds struggle with decision-making because their brain's stress response remains active. The amygdala, which processes fear and emotion, can hijack logical thinking, making every decision feel riskier than it actually is.

People who have experienced significant emotional wounds are more likely to make avoidance-based decisions, opting for the least emotionally taxing choice rather than the one that leads to growth. In other words, pain keeps us stuck in cycles of self-protection rather than progress.

WHEN THE HEAD AND GUT SAY YES, BUT THE HEART SAYS NO

This internal conflict is incredibly frustrating. Your head has logically analyzed the situation and sees no reason not to move forward. Your gut is pushing you toward action, sensing excitement or instinctive alignment, but your heart refuses to cooperate.

Physically, this might feel like the following:

- a tight chest, as if something is weighing on you
- a lump in your throat, like there are unspoken words you can't release
- a feeling of heaviness as if every step forward takes extra effort

Mentally, this conflict manifests as the following:

- fear of repeating past pain or wondering if history will repeat itself
- self-sabotage by finding ways to delay, overcomplicate, or talk yourself out of things
- emotional outbursts or shutdowns, bringing moments of intense overwhelm or total disconnection

People often say the following:

- "It hurts too much."
- "I'm so angry."
- "I feel overwhelmed."
- "I can't think."

These are all signs that the heart is still holding onto pain that needs to be acknowledged before the decision-making process can move forward.

JASON AND THE WEIGHT OF UNPROCESSED PAIN

Jason came to me wanting to sharpen his business and leadership skills, but he felt stuck. No matter how hard he worked, he kept hitting the same walls. As we explored his story, we uncovered a past romantic relationship that had deeply wounded him. He had never processed the heartbreak. He buried it beneath relentless ambition, hoping success would erase the pain. In fact, when I asked about the relationship, he seemed almost uninterested in talking about it and more motivated to *get to the point* of increasing his momentum in life.

But pain doesn't go away when we ignore it. It just gets redirected. In Jason's case, his unresolved hurt was affecting his leadership. It made him second-guess himself. It made him put too much pressure on performance. Most of all, it dulled his natural joy and energy, making him so magnetic in his efforts. For the first time, he allowed himself to process his pain with me and put words to the heavy emotion he was carrying. Sometimes, processing pain involves words, often it involves tears, and sometimes it even requires grief. For Jason, he had to engage with all of these. Once he did, the transformation was quickly visible and is ongoing. He no longer approached leadership from a wounded state. He began to build relationships, take strategic risks, and experience success like never before. His healing changed everything.

BIBLICAL WISDOM ON THE HEART

Proverbs 4:23 says, "Above all else, guard your heart, for everything you do flows from it" (NIV). This verse reminds us that our heart's condition impacts every area of our lives, including our decisions. When we carry unresolved pain, it affects how we engage with the world. The heart signal, if ignored, will interrupt everything. I often think of the heart as an inner child. It's not the thinking part of me; it's the *feeling* part of me. If that inner child starts to scream and cry, most of us either try to indulge it or silence it to eliminate the pain. The wise response is to learn to acknowledge the heart signal and address it with care because everything else flows from it.

Jesus modeled emotional wisdom. He wept at the loss of his friend Lazarus, showing us that acknowledging grief is part of healing (John 11:35). He also challenged people to move beyond their wounds, asking the man at the pool of Bethesda, "Do you want to be healed?" (John 5:6).

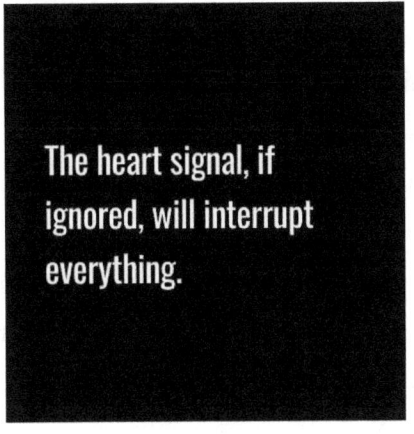

The heart signal, if ignored, will interrupt everything.

Healing requires willingness. We cannot stay in our pain forever.

TOOLS TO OVERCOME A HESITANT HEART

1. **Healing begins with acknowledgment:** We cannot heal what we refuse to name. When your heart is holding you back, start by recognizing the emotions at play. What are you actually feeling? Is it grief, anger, disappointment, or fear? Name it. Emotional clarity brings power.

2. **Allow yourself to express the emotion:** Emoting isn't weakness; it's how we release stored pain. Whether through journaling, talking with a trusted friend, or professional counseling, expressing emotions helps us move through them rather than being trapped by them.

Each emotion has a healthy response that leads to healing. Sadness needs comfort. Allow yourself to receive support. Anger needs change. Identify what needs to shift. Loneliness needs connection. Seek out meaningful relationships. The list goes on, but if we learn to look at emotions as informants to our needs, we can process them much differently.

3. **Recognize that healing is not about forgetting the pain but reframing it:** Your hurt is part of your story, but it doesn't have to define your future. By processing emotional wounds rather than avoiding them, your heart signal can once again guide you in a healthy, constructive way.

When the heart holds us back, it's not because it's trying to stop us from living. It's because it's trying to protect us from experiencing pain again. But true healing doesn't come from avoiding risk. It comes from facing the hurt, processing it, and choosing to move forward with strength, wisdom, and wholeness.

If your heart is hesitant, ask yourself: *Am I making this decision based on reality, or am I letting old wounds dictate my future?* Healing your heart won't erase the past, but it will open the door to a future where your decisions are no longer driven by pain but by purpose.

PERSONAL REFLECTIONS - WHEN YOUR HEART HOLDS YOU BACK (HURT)

1. Have I ever experienced a moment when my heart signal was holding me back from something my head and gut were saying yes to? What was the outcome?
2. Do I tend to emotionally shut down or emotionally flood when faced with pain? How has this affected my decision-making in the past?
3. Is there a particular hurt from my past that I have not fully processed? How does it impact my current relationships, career, or self-perception?
4. What small step can I take today to begin healing emotional wounds that may be holding me back from making confident, healthy decisions?

CHAPTER 8

WHEN YOUR GUT HOLDS YOU BACK (FEAR)

"Do one thing every day that scares you."
—Eleanor Roosevelt

WHEN YOUR GUT HOLDS YOU BACK (FEAR)

THERE'S a kind of fear that doesn't just sit in your mind; it burrows deep into your gut, gnawing at you and making it impossible to think straight, let alone make clear decisions. I felt that fear the day my son, Malachi, got really sick. What started as the flu and strep throat spiraled into a rare post-viral condition and reaction called erythema multiforme. His skin broke out in an extreme rash, his joints swelled until he couldn't walk, and his breathing became labored.

The doctors assured us after thorough checks that he would be okay and that it would clear up eventually. But the days that followed were some of the longest of my life. Watching him painfully unable to move, wincing at the slightest movement, or hearing the faintest noise from his room would send my gut into turmoil. My mind knew he was on the path to recovery. My heart longed to believe it. But my gut was drowning in fear. I was constantly on edge, unable to focus, reacting to every sound as if it signaled catastrophe.

That's the power of gut-level fear. It hijacks your instincts and holds you hostage, even when everything else is telling you it's okay to move forward. And when that fear isn't addressed, it begins to seep into every decision, creating an invisible barrier between you and the life you want to live.

THE PROBLEM: FEAR AS AN OVERACTIVE GUT SIGNAL

The gut signal is where our instincts live. It helps us sense danger, trust our intuition, and make quick, decisive moves. But when the gut is overwhelmed by fear, those instincts become skewed. Instead of guiding us wisely, fear distorts our perception of risk, amplifies doubts, and keeps us stuck in cycles of hesitation.

When the gut holds someone back, it often shows up as hesitancy, anxiety, insecurity, or even physical symptoms like nausea, tension, or loss of appetite. It's that feeling of dread that rises in your stomach before a big decision. This fear often whispers, *What if it all goes wrong?* and convinces us that inaction is the safest option.

The tricky part is that fear often masquerades as wisdom. We tell ourselves we're being cautious or prudent when, in reality, we're avoiding discomfort. Fear convinces us that staying where we are, even if we're miserable, is safer than stepping into the unknown. But the truth is, unchecked fear keeps us from growth, holding us back from opportunities that could  transform our lives. It creates a false sense of security that traps us in the familiar, even when the familiar is unfulfilling.

THE SCIENCE OF FEAR AND DECISION PARALYSIS

Fear isn't just an emotion; it's a biological response. The gut, often referred to as the "second brain," contains the enteric nervous system, which communicates directly with the brain via the vagus nerve. This system is responsible for the "gut feelings" we experience, especially under stress.

When fear takes hold, the body's fight-flight-freeze response is activated. The amygdala, the brain's fear center, sends signals that trigger the release of stress hormones like cortisol and adrenaline. This floods the body with physical symptoms, such as a racing heart, shallow breathing, tightened muscles, and that familiar feeling of a twisted stomach.

Chronic fear can cause temporary discomfort and alter our decision-making process. People who operate under prolonged stress or fear are more likely to make avoidance-based decisions, choosing the path of least resistance rather than the one that leads to growth. This can manifest as procrastination, indecisiveness, or abandoning opportunities altogether. Leaders who live with chronic fear are not able to make clear decisions because they live in constant risk avoidance and self-preservation.

Interestingly, the gut's microbiome, the trillions of bacteria living in our digestive tract, also plays a role in how we process fear and stress. Research indicates that an unhealthy gut can exacerbate anxiety and stress responses, creating a feedback loop where fear affects not only our decisions but also our physical health. This mind-gut connection underscores the importance of addressing fear both mentally and physically.

WHEN THE HEAD AND HEART SAY YES, BUT THE GUT SAYS NO

Few things are more frustrating than feeling fully aligned in your head and heart, only to have your gut pump the brakes. Your head has analyzed the situation and sees the logic in moving forward. Your heart is emotionally invested, feeling the excitement or passion for the opportunity. But your gut is screaming, *What if this goes wrong?*

Physically, this might feel like the following:

- a churning stomach or nausea, like your body is rejecting the idea of moving forward
- loss of appetite; even if you're hungry, you can't eat
- restlessness or trouble sleeping
- sweaty palms or a dry mouth

Mentally, this conflict often sounds like the following:

- "I don't know why, but something feels off."
- "What if I fail?"
- "This just seems risky."
- "What if everything falls apart?"
- "I'm not ready for this."

This kind of gut-level fear can paralyze us, even when every other part of us is ready to take the leap. It's important to recognize when this fear is protecting us from real danger versus when it's holding us back from necessary growth. Often, the discomfort is a sign that we're on the brink of something transformative but only if we can push through the fear.

KYLE AND THE FEAR OF FUTURE FAILURE

Kyle came to me in the middle of a major career pressure. He was excelling in an unexpected and unprecedented business outlet in the creative space for himself. His talent and skill garnered him many great opportunities and deals in his space. However, it felt tumultuous based on the up-and-down nature of his digital work. His head knew he was doing well. His heart was passionate about the vision. His gut, however, was twisted up in fear.

Kyle worried about the risks. What if he failed? How would it affect his family? This led to emotional frustration each time things didn't go as well as he had planned. It wasn't that he didn't want to move forward. He just couldn't shake the fear of future failure. This fear started to seep into other areas of his life. He found himself more distracted, less engaged with his natural, outgoing, creative qualities, and constantly distracted by "what if" scenarios that never came to pass.

Together, we unpacked his fear. We explored what he was afraid of and why he was afraid. It wasn't about the business; it was about his fear of failure defining him as a man, a father, and a provider. His work was deeply personal, and so the performance of it felt personal too. Once he realized this, he was able to reframe his perspective. We used a technique called fear-setting to map out the worst-case scenarios and create action plans for them. Even if one plan failed miserably, there'd be other opportunities. I'll never forget how he acknowledged the revenue and performance he viewed as unacceptable today would have been unbelievable success to him a year prior. This reminder gave him a sense of control over the unknown.

When he took this resolved confidence into his work, it made a world of difference. Kyle found not only success but fulfillment because he refused to let fear dictate his decisions. Protecting that fulfillment meant fighting fear amid success. More importantly, he learned that courage isn't the absence of fear; it's the decision to move forward despite it.

BIBLICAL WISDOM ON OVERCOMING FEAR

Fear isn't from God. The verse in 2 Timothy 1:7 reminds us, "For God has not given us a spirit of fear, but of power and of love and of a sound mind" (NKJV). Fear clouds our instincts, but faith clarifies them. This verse is a powerful reminder that while fear may feel overwhelming, it doesn't have to control us.

Take Gideon from the Book of Judges. Gideon was terrified when God called him to lead Israel against the Midianites. He doubted himself, asking for multiple signs before taking action. He even hid from his calling at first, convinced he wasn't capable. But even in his fear, he eventually obeyed, trusting that God's strength was greater than his weakness. Gideon's victory wasn't just about defeating the Midianites but overcoming the fear that had paralyzed him for so long.

Similarly, throughout Scripture, we see figures like Moses, who doubted his ability to lead, and Esther, who risked her life to save her people, confront their fears and step into their purpose. These stories remind us that fear is a natural part of the journey, but it doesn't have to be the final word.

TOOLS TO OVERCOME FEAR-BASED GUT SIGNALS

1. **Fear-setting:** Instead of avoiding fear, confront it head-on. Identify the worst-case scenario and make a plan for what you would do if it happened. By preparing for the worst, you reduce its power over you. This technique helps transform vague, overwhelming fears into manageable, specific concerns.

2. **Seek encouragement:** Surround yourself with people who have faced similar fears and succeeded. Hearing their stories can help normalize fear and inspire confidence. Sometimes, knowing that others have walked the same path and come out stronger can be the encouragement you need to take the first step.

3. **Talk it out:** Verbalizing fear helps diminish its grip. Whether with a coach, mentor, or friend, talking through your fears allows you to see them more objectively. Often, just hearing your fears spoken aloud reveals how irrational they are.

4. **Take small steps:** You don't have to leap all at once. Break big decisions into smaller, manageable steps to build confidence and momentum. Each small win reinforces your ability to handle the next challenge.
5. **Reframe the narrative:** Shift from "What if I fail?" to "What if I succeed?" Focus on the potential for growth rather than the fear of failure. Reframing fear as an opportunity for growth changes the way you approach challenges.
6. **Mindfulness and breathing techniques:** Fear often manifests physically, so engaging in mindfulness practices or deep-breathing exercises can help calm the body's stress response. This physical calmness can lead to clearer thinking and better decision-making.
7. **Visualize success:** Spend time imagining what success looks and feels like. Visualization can help rewire your brain to focus on positive outcomes rather than dwelling on worst-case scenarios.

When the gut holds us back, it's usually trying to protect us from perceived danger. But not all danger is real. Sometimes, it's just discomfort disguised as risk. Learning to discern between healthy caution and paralyzing fear is key to making confident decisions.

If your gut is hesitating, ask yourself: *Is this fear protecting me from real harm, or is it keeping me from growth?* Trust that you have the power to move forward even when fear tries to hold you back.

Fear may be a passenger on the journey, but it doesn't have to be the driver.

PERSONAL REFLECTIONS – WHEN YOUR GUT HOLDS YOU BACK (FEAR)

1. Have I experienced a time when my gut fear held me back, even though my head and heart were aligned? What was the outcome?
2. What recurring fears hold me back from taking risks or stepping into new opportunities?
3. In what ways has fear affected my personal growth or relationships? Are there areas of my life where fear is still influencing my decisions?
4. What small, manageable step can I take today toward a decision I've been avoiding because of fear?

PART THREE

NO, BUT...

"It is not hard to make decisions when you know what your values are."
—Roy E. Disney

PART THREE: NO, BUT...

THE TEMPTATION TO SAY YES WHEN YOU SHOULDN'T

We've all experienced standing at the crossroads of a decision, feeling like everything in us is saying no, except for that one persistent voice pushing us to go for it. It's like having two friends waving red flags in your face while the third is shouting, "What's the worst that could happen?" Sometimes that lone signal feels so compelling, so convincing, that we ignore the louder, more rational chorus of "no" echoing from the rest of our being.

The Decision Code gives a framework for this conflict: When two out of three signals are telling you no, it's probably wise to listen. That's why this part of the book is about recognizing those moments when your decision-making signals are out of sync and learning how to resist the urge to say yes when the smarter choice is no.

> When two out of three signals are telling you no, it's probably wise to listen.

While Part Two focuses on the inner conflict that arises when one signal holds you back from a decision you're mostly aligned with, Part Three dives into the opposite scenario. These are the times when your head, heart, and gut aren't at war. They're practically unanimous in their decision to say no, except for that one rogue signal trying to convince you otherwise.

This is where decision-making gets tricky. That single signal can be incredibly persuasive, making you question your better judgment. If you're not careful, it can lead you down paths you'll wish you never took. So, why do we feel pulled to say yes when we know we shouldn't, and how can we recognize when that pull is leading us astray?

THE DECISION CODE: RECOGNIZING THE ROGUE SIGNAL

The Decision Code is about tuning into the signals from your head (logic), heart (emotion), and gut (instinct) and understanding how they interplay in your decision-making process. When all three signals align, decisions feel easy and natural. When they conflict, as we explored in Part Two, it can cause indecision and hesitation.

What happens when only one signal is pushing you forward while the other two are clearly saying no? That's where the real challenge lies. It's like one part of you is shouting over the rest, trying to convince you to ignore the warning signs. These rogue signals can be powerful, but they're often misleading.

In this section, we'll explore three common scenarios where a single signal tries to lead the charge and why it's important to pause and reconsider before following that impulse:

1. **When only the head says yes (apathy):** This happens when you're making decisions purely based on logic, yet your heart and gut are screaming, *No!* You might rationalize a decision because it makes sense on paper, but emotionally and instinctively, it feels wrong. This can lead

to apathy, a disconnection from your emotions and instincts, resulting in choices that lack meaning or fulfillment.

2. **When only the heart says yes (emotionalism):** Here, your emotions are running the show. Your heart is all in, but your head and gut know better. This kind of decision-making can lead to emotionally charged choices that don't hold up under scrutiny. It's easy to get swept up in the moment, but when the emotional high fades, you're left dealing with the consequences.

3. **When only the gut says yes (impulsiveness):** Sometimes your instincts are pushing you toward a decision, even when your head and heart are waving warning flags. This gut-driven impulsiveness can lead to rash decisions that feel right in the moment but lack the support of careful thought or emotional grounding.

WHY THAT ONE SIGNAL FEELS SO COMPELLING

You might be wondering, *Why is that one signal so hard to ignore?* The answer lies in how we're wired. Each of our decision-making centers—head, heart, and gut—has unique strengths and weaknesses. Depending on your personality, experiences, and even your dominant decision-making style, you might naturally lean on one signal more than the others.

For example, if you're a head-dominant person, you might find it easy to rationalize decisions, even when they don't feel right emotionally or instinctively. If you're heart-dominant, your emotions might overpower logic and caution, leading you to make choices based on how you feel rather than what makes sense. And if you're gut-dominant, your instincts might push you to act quickly without fully considering the consequences.

These tendencies aren't inherently bad. They're part of what makes you unique. However, problems arise when one signal starts to dominate the decision-making process while ignoring the wisdom of the other two. It's like trying to drive a car with one flat tire. You might still move forward, but the ride will be rough, and you're more likely to crash.

LEARNING TO SAY NO WITH CONFIDENCE

The goal of this section isn't just to help you recognize when a rogue signal is leading you astray but to empower you to say no with confidence. Sometimes the hardest thing to do is to walk away from something that feels tempting. But when you learn to trust the signals from your head, heart, and gut and recognize when one is out of balance, you'll find it easier to make decisions that align with your values and goals.

Each of the next three chapters will delve deep into these scenarios, sharing stories, strategies, and insights to help you navigate the tricky waters of decision-making when your signals are out of sync. We'll explore how to recognize when your head is leading you into apathy, when your heart is leading you into emotionalism, and when your gut is leading you into impulsiveness.

By the end of this section, you'll have a clearer understanding of how to listen to all three signals and make decisions that are balanced, thoughtful, and intentional. You'll recognize when to say no, even if one part of you is screaming yes. You'll have the tools to make choices that lead to growth, fulfillment, and peace of mind.

CHAPTER 9

WHEN ONLY YOUR HEAD PUSHES YOU (APATHY)

"Reason without emotion is blind; emotion without reason is empty."
—Immanuel Kant

WHEN ONLY YOUR HEAD PUSHES YOU (APATHY)

I once made a decision that, on paper, seemed perfectly logical. I chose a master's degree program in seminary that was unnecessarily rigorous. It was the kind of program that demanded relentless academic effort. The strange thing is I was already pastoring. I didn't need that degree for my role, and deep down, I knew it. My head told me it made sense, that the recognition would be worth it, and that it was the right step to advance my credentials, but my heart and gut weren't in it—at all.

As each semester passed, I felt more and more detached. What started as excitement about the intellectual challenge quickly turned into apathy. I found myself going through the motions, showing up for classes without passion, and completing assignments with minimal engagement. My heart felt distant, my gut screamed that I was on the wrong path, but my mind kept rationalizing, *This is what you're supposed to do.*

Eventually, I reached my breaking point. I switched programs, choosing a counseling degree that aligned with my passions and purpose. It was like a breath of fresh air. I felt reconnected to myself, energized by the work, and more authentic in my pursuits. That shift wasn't about academics. It was escaping the trap of apathy and finding my way back to wholehearted living.

THE PROBLEM: WHEN LOGIC TAKES OVER AND APATHY CREEPS IN

Apathy in decision-making isn't just about feeling indifferent; it's about disconnecting from the parts of yourself that bring meaning and fulfillment. When only your head is pushing you forward, decisions become sterile and stripped of emotion and instinct. You're left following a logical path that might make sense on paper but leaves you feeling empty inside. Discernment comes from clarity, but apathy comes from burnout.

This isn't just about big life choices, either. Apathy can creep into the smallest of decisions, slowly draining the joy and excitement from your daily life. It's the numbness you feel when you're stuck in a job solely for the paycheck, even though it drains your soul. It's the disengagement of staying in a dating relationship because it's comfortable, even though your heart knows it's over. It's the disconnection that occurs when you pursue goals that look impressive from the outside but don't resonate with who you truly are.

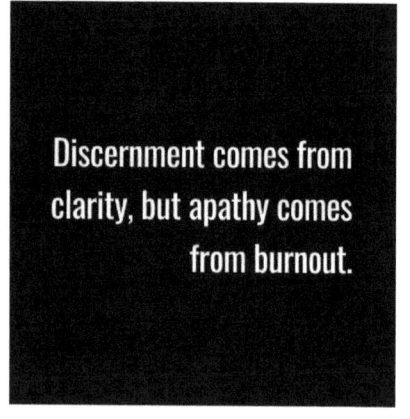

Discernment comes from clarity, but apathy comes from burnout.

When apathy takes over, life feels like a series of obligations rather than opportunities. You're not living—you're surviving. The more you rely solely on your head to make decisions, the more you risk falling into this emotional dead zone. Over time, this can lead to burnout, frustration, and a profound sense of emptiness.

WHAT APATHY LOOKS AND FEELS LIKE

When you're making decisions from a head-only place, the signs are hard to miss if you're paying attention. Often, though, people caught in this cycle don't even realize it. They're so used to operating from logic that they've tuned out the signals from their heart and gut.

The following feelings can be signs of apathy:

- Numbness: You feel emotionally flat, unable to connect with joy, excitement, or even frustration.
- Disengagement: You go through the motions without feeling truly present in your work, relationships, or daily activities.
- Boredom: Even activities you once loved feel dull and uninspiring.
- Disconnection: You feel out of touch with your needs, desires, and passions.
- Distraction and escapism: You may turn to vices like overworking, mindless scrolling, or unhealthy habits to fill the void left by emotional detachment.

You might have the following thoughts:

- *It makes sense, but I'm just not feeling it.*
- *I'm doing what I'm supposed to, but I'm not happy.*
- *I'm bored but can't afford to change things.*

These are clear indicators that your decision-making process is out of balance and that it's time to reconnect with your heart and gut.

THE SCIENCE BEHIND APATHY AND COGNITIVE OVERLOAD

Apathy is more than a mindset; it's a neurological state. When we rely solely on cognitive reasoning, we overactivate areas of the brain, like the PFC, which is responsible for logic, analysis, and executive function. While this part of the brain is essential for decision-making, over-reliance on it can lead to cognitive overload and emotional detachment.

Studies have shown that prolonged cognitive strain without emotional engagement can result in decision fatigue and mental burnout.[1] When you're constantly making decisions based on logic alone, your brain becomes exhausted, leading to a sense of detachment and indifference.

Moreover, apathy is linked to decreased activity in the brain's reward system. When decisions are made without emotional or instinctual input, they lack the dopamine-driven satisfaction that comes from meaningful, fulfilling choices. This lack of emotional reward reinforces the cycle of apathy, making it harder to break free.

WHEN THE HEAD SAYS YES, BUT THE HEART AND GUT SAY NO

When your head is the only part of you pushing forward, it can feel like you're on autopilot. You're making decisions that seem rational, but something feels off. Your heart isn't in it, and your gut is quietly protesting, but your mind keeps pushing, saying, *This is the logical thing to do.*

This conflict may manifest in the following physical and emotional symptoms:

- Restlessness: You can't seem to settle into your decisions, constantly questioning if you're on the right path.
- Lack of motivation: Even though the decision makes sense, you struggle to find the energy to follow through.
- Emotional numbness: You feel disconnected from your desires and passions, going through the motions without real engagement.
- Physical fatigue: The mental effort of pushing forward without emotional or instinctual support can leave you feeling drained and exhausted.

This disconnect can be deeply frustrating. You might find yourself thinking, *Why am I doing this if it doesn't make me happy?* or *Why does this feel so empty, even though it's the right thing to do?*

REBECCA AND THE BURNOUT OF LOGIC-DRIVEN LIVING

Rebecca was an entrepreneur who came to me on the brink of burnout. She was aggressively pushing her brand and business, driven by a relentless work ethic and a sharp, logical mind. On the surface, everything looked great. Her business was thriving, her revenue was growing, and she was hitting every milestone she'd set.

Beneath the surface, however, Rebecca was struggling. Her emotions kept flaring up in unexpected ways, and her body was shutting down. She was exhausted, irritable, and disconnected from the passion that had once fueled her work. But her logical, business-oriented mind kept pushing her to keep going, generate more revenue, and stick to the plan.

Through our work together, Rebecca realized that her head had been running the show for too long. She had ignored the signals from her heart and gut, convincing herself that logic and hard work were all that mattered, but that approach had left her emotionally depleted and physically burned out.

When Rebecca finally paused to listen to her heart and gut, she realized she needed a complete shift in her work and her soul. She took time off to rest, recover, and reconnect with her passions. She redefined her approach to business, focusing on work that brought her joy and fulfillment rather than just financial success. The result? A dramatic resurgence of her energy, creativity, and overall well-being. Rebecca saved her business and reconnected with herself in the process.

BIBLICAL WISDOM: RUNNING WITH PURPOSE

The Bible offers profound insight into the dangers of living a head-only, logic-driven life. In 1 Corinthians 9:26, Paul writes, "Therefore I do not run like someone running aimlessly; I do not fight like a boxer beating the air" (NIV). This verse contrasts those who live with purpose and passion against those who go through the motions without direction or meaning.

Relying solely on logic can make us like athletes who run aimlessly, expending energy without a clear sense of purpose. True fulfillment comes from aligning our decisions with our head, heart, and gut and living with intention and authenticity.

TOOLS TO OVERCOME APATHY AND RECONNECT WITH PURPOSE

1. **Take a break:** Sometimes, the best thing you can do is step away. Give yourself permission to rest and recharge. This isn't lazy. It's a necessary reset to reconnect with your heart and gut.
2. **Get back in touch with your body:** Physical movement is a powerful way to break free from apathy. Engage in activities that get you out of your head and into your body, whether it's exercise, dancing, or simply taking a walk in nature.
3. **Reclaim your sleep and playfulness:** Sleep isn't just for physical recovery; it's essential for emotional and mental well-being. Prioritize rest and make time for play, creativity, and activities that bring you joy.
4. **Revisit your dreams and desires:** Take time to reflect on your passions and goals. Are you living in alignment with what truly matters to you? If not, what changes can you make to reconnect with your purpose?

5. **Practice mindful decision-making**: Slow down your decision-making process to include emotional and instinctual input. Ask yourself, *How does this feel?* and *Does this align with my values and passions?*
6. **Seek support**: Don't navigate this alone. Talk to a trusted friend, mentor, or counselor who can help you explore your feelings and reconnect with what matters most.

When only the head is pushing you forward, it's easy to fall into the trap of apathy. You're living a life that looks good on the outside but feels empty on the inside. True fulfillment comes from aligning your logic, emotions, and instincts to make decisions that resonate with your whole being.

If you find yourself feeling numb, disconnected, or stuck in a cycle of going through the motions, it's time to pause and listen to the signals from your heart and gut. Reconnect with what brings you joy, passion, and purpose. Life isn't just about making the right decisions on paper. It's about making decisions that lead to a life worth living.

> True fulfillment comes from aligning your logic, emotions, and instincts to make decisions that resonate with your whole being.

PERSONAL REFLECTIONS – WHEN ONLY YOUR HEAD PUSHES YOU (APATHY)

1. Have I ever made a decision based purely on logic, even though my heart and gut were signaling no? What was the outcome of that decision?
2. Do I recognize moments in my life where I've felt numb, disengaged, or disconnected from my choices? What might have caused that apathy?
3. When was the last time I felt truly energized and connected to a decision? What signals were my heart and gut giving me at that time?
4. What dreams or desires have I put on hold because they didn't seem logical or practical? How might I revisit them now?

CHAPTER 10

WHEN ONLY YOUR HEART PUSHES YOU (EMOTIONALISM)

"Feelings are great servants, but terrible masters."
—Dallas Willard

WHEN ONLY YOUR HEART PUSHES YOU (EMOTIONALISM)

I'VE always been more head-dominant in my decision-making, but even I've fallen victim to emotional pulls I couldn't rationalize. Case in point: those infamous timeshare presentations. You know, the ones that lure you in with the promise of free tickets or a "free" vacation, but the real goal is to get you emotionally hooked. I sat through one of those presentations certain that it wouldn't work on me, and I have to admit, they knew exactly how to tug at my heartstrings.

They painted vivid pictures of family vacations, my kid laughing on the beach, roasting marshmallows by the campfire, and creating lifelong memories. The whole thing was designed to bypass logic and go straight for the heart. Even though my head was screaming, *This is a terrible financial decision,* and my gut was whispering, *This doesn't feel right,* the emotional pull was strong. They tapped into the guilt of not doing enough for my family, of missing out on precious memories.

I didn't buy the timeshare (thankfully), but it is a perfect example of how easily emotions can take the wheel. When the heart is the only signal pushing us forward, it can lead to decisions we later regret, not because they weren't heartfelt but because they ignored the wisdom of logic and instinct.

THE PROBLEM: WHEN EMOTIONS OVERRULE EVERYTHING ELSE

Emotionalism in decision-making isn't about being emotional. It's about letting emotions completely dictate your choices, even when your head and gut are signaling caution. It's reacting to overwhelming feelings, whether it's guilt, comparison, infatuation, or even anger, and letting those feelings drive you into decisions that don't align with your deeper values or logic.

Emotionalism is when you're so flooded by emotion that you can't see clearly. It's saying yes to things because you don't want to disappoint others, overcommitting out of guilt, or staying in unhealthy relationships because you're afraid of hurting someone's feelings. It's when your emotions scream so loudly that you can't hear the rational voice of your head or the intuitive warnings of your gut.

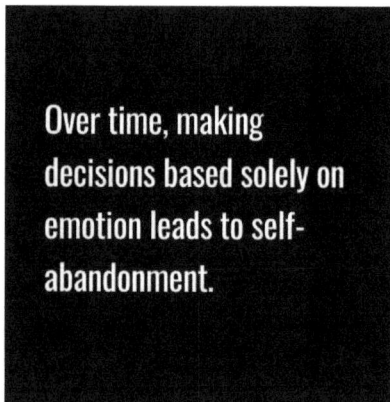

Over time, making decisions based solely on emotion leads to self-abandonment.

Over time, making decisions based solely on emotion leads to self-abandonment. You lose sight of your own needs, values, and instincts, all in the name of keeping others happy or avoiding uncomfortable feelings. While these decisions might bring temporary relief or satisfaction, they often lead to regret, frustration, and burnout in the long run.

WHAT EMOTIONALISM LOOKS AND FEELS LIKE

When you're making heart-only decisions, you might experience the following physical and emotional signs:

- Intense emotional swings: Your feelings dictate your decisions, leading to highs and lows that feel like a roller coaster.
- Emotional flooding: You feel overwhelmed by emotions, unable to think clearly or rationally.
- Physical sensations: Strong emotions can manifest as tightness in the chest or a racing heart.
- Tears or outbursts: Even small decisions can trigger disproportionate emotional reactions.

You might have the following thoughts:

- *It just feels right, even if it doesn't make sense.*
- *I know it's not logical, but I can't help how I feel.*
- *I'll regret it if I don't do this, even though it's risky.*

When emotions take over, it's easy to mistake them for truth. But emotions are signals, not facts. They're important to acknowledge, but they need to be balanced with logic and instinct to make wise decisions.

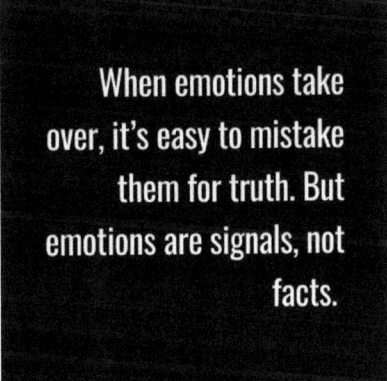

When emotions take over, it's easy to mistake them for truth. But emotions are signals, not facts.

WHEN THE HEART SAYS YES, BUT THE HEAD AND GUT SAY NO

When your heart is the only signal pushing you forward, it can feel like you're caught in an emotional current that's hard to resist. Your head might recognize the risks, and your gut might sense something's off, but the emotional pull is so strong that you ignore those signals.

Physically and emotionally, this conflict might show up in the following ways:

- Overwhelm: You feel emotionally flooded, unable to think clearly or assess the situation logically.
- Physical tension: Emotions manifest in your body as tightness in the chest or a racing heart.
- Guilt or obligation: You feel compelled to act out of guilt, comparison, or the desire to please others, even if it doesn't align with your values.
- Emotional fatigue: You consistently make decisions based on emotions, which can leave you feeling drained, especially when things don't turn out as you hoped.

You might find yourself thinking, *I know this isn't the smartest choice, but I feel like I have to do it,* or *It hurts too much to say no, even though I know I should.*

JUAN AND THE STRUGGLE TO REBUILD LOVE

Juan came to me after a devastating divorce from his wife, Maria, following her infidelity. As a head-dominant individual, he initially approached the situation with logic, trying to process what had happened and how to move forward. But emotions don't always play by the rules of logic.

After some time, Juan and Maria began interacting again. She was earnestly trying to make amends, and Juan forgave her. Logically, he could see that Maria had done the work to rebuild trust. His gut instinct told him it was safe to trust her again. But his heart kept flaring up at the thought of being hurt again, and it was pushing him to run away from her. The emotional trauma of betrayal was so strong that it clouded his ability to move forward, even though his head and gut were aligned.

We spent a lot of time not only talking about the betrayal but also processing the emotions tied to it. It wasn't enough to think it through. Juan had to feel his way through the pain. Eventually, as he worked through the emotional wounds, his heart began to align with his head and gut. Juan and Maria remarried, and their relationship is now stronger than ever. But it wouldn't have happened if Juan hadn't faced his hesitant emotions directly and learned to balance them with logic and instinct.

BIBLICAL WISDOM: GUARDING THE HEART WITHOUT IGNORING IT

The Bible acknowledges the power of the heart in decision-making as the source from which all life flows. Biblical wisdom recognizes that the heart is central to who we are. But it also warns against letting unguarded emotions lead us astray.

Emotions are a gift, but they need to be balanced with wisdom. When we let our hearts run unchecked, we risk making decisions that feel right in the moment but lead to regret later. Guarding the heart means acknowledging our emotions, processing them, and ensuring they align with our values and purpose.

> **Guarding the heart means acknowledging our emotions, processing them, and ensuring they align with our values and purpose.**

TOOLS TO OVERCOME EMOTIONALISM AND BALANCE DECISION-MAKING

1. **Process the emotion, don't suppress it:** Emotions must be felt and processed, not ignored. Use creative outlets like journaling, art, or music to express what you're feeling.

2. **Slow down your decision-making:** Give yourself time to let intense emotions settle before making big decisions. What feels urgent in the heat of the moment often looks different after some reflection.

3. **Engage in physical outlets:** Physical movement can help process emotions stored in the body. Whether it's exercise, yoga, or even a simple walk, moving your body can help release emotional tension.

4. **Seek perspective:** Talk to trusted friends, mentors, or counselors who can offer objective insight. An outside perspective can sometimes help balance emotional responses with logic and instinct.
5. **Identify the root of the emotion:** Ask yourself, *Why am I feeling this so strongly? Is it guilt, fear of disappointing others, or unresolved past experiences?* Understanding the root can help you navigate the emotion more effectively.

When only the heart is pushing you forward, it's easy to get swept up in the intensity of your emotions. But emotions, while powerful, are only one part of the decision-making process. True wisdom comes from balancing your heart, head, and gut to make choices that are thoughtful, grounded, and aligned with your values.

If you find yourself making decisions based solely on how you feel, it's time to pause and listen to the other signals. Honor your emotions, but don't let them lead you into decisions that don't serve your long-term well-being. By balancing emotion with logic and instinct, you'll make decisions that feel right and stand the test of time.

PERSONAL REFLECTIONS – WHEN ONLY YOUR HEART PUSHES YOU (EMOTIONALISM)

1. Have I ever made a decision purely based on emotion, even when my head and gut were signaling caution? What was the outcome, and how did I feel afterward?
2. Have I overcommitted or said yes to something just to avoid disappointing others? What were the long-term effects on my well-being?
3. In what situations do I find it hardest to balance my emotions with logic and gut instincts? Why do I think that is?
4. How can I guard my heart in future decision-making, ensuring my emotions are acknowledged but not the sole driver of my choices?

CHAPTER 11

WHEN ONLY YOUR GUT PUSHES YOU (IMPULSIVENESS)

"Freedom is not the absence of commitments, but the ability to choose —and commit—to what is best."
—Paulo Coelho

WHEN ONLY YOUR GUT PUSHES YOU (IMPULSIVENESS)

LONG before my wife and I were married, we were in what we now jokingly refer to as a "friendlationship." It was that weird in-between space where we were close friends, but it was painfully obvious that she had feelings for me. Everyone could see we were supposed to be together, except for me. If you didn't know, church people have a keen ability to offer up unsolicited opinions about your love life.

One day, I finally had enough of the comments about us and the feeling that she was hoping we'd get together. I had this overwhelming gut reaction that said, *You need to shut this down. Right now.* Without thinking it through, without consulting my heart or my head, I told her that despite whatever feelings she had for me, we would never be together romantically. Yes, I said, "Never."

Logically, I knew she was an ideal potential partner. My head saw all the reasons why we would make a great team. My heart? Oh, my heart loved the bond we shared. But my gut was screaming that I needed to take control, to stop something that felt like it was being decided for me. So, I impulsively shut it down.

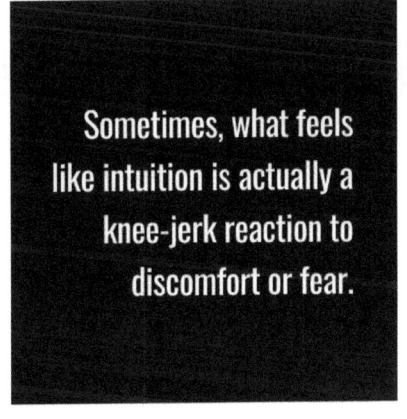

Sometimes, what feels like intuition is actually a knee-jerk reaction to discomfort or fear.

Thankfully, she was more gracious than I deserved. She stayed patient and maintained our friendship. And guess what? Five months later, I asked her to be my girlfriend. Now, we're married, and I'm thankful every day that she didn't take my impulsive gut reaction at face value.

This experience taught me something profound about gut-driven decisions. Sometimes, what feels like intuition is actually a knee-jerk reaction to discomfort or fear. My gut wasn't warning me about Amanda; it was reacting to the pressure of others and the fear of decision. That's the tricky thing about impulsiveness. It masquerades as instinct when, in reality, it's often a cover for something deeper.

IMPULSIVENESS OVERRIDES EVERYTHING ELSE

When your gut is the only signal pushing you forward, it can lead to fast, reactive, and often reckless decisions. Impulsiveness isn't just about making quick decisions. It's about acting without giving yourself the space to think logically or process emotionally. It's giving in to urges or reactions that feel primal, lustful, aggressive, or explosive.

Impulsiveness often thrives in moments of discomfort or uncertainty. When faced with situations that make us anxious, bored, or vulnerable, our gut can scream for immediate action as a way to escape those feelings. It's like our internal wiring gets hijacked by the need for instant gratification or relief.

Sometimes, impulsiveness feels like a force you can't resist. It's like trying to keep a basketball underwater, but it just keeps resurfacing. You might feel like you'll explode if you don't act right now. But just because the urge feels strong doesn't mean it's leading you in the right direction. In fact, acting on impulse can often pull us further away from our goals and values.

When impulsiveness is in the driver's seat, it often leads to decisions that might satisfy a momentary craving but result in long-term regret. It's jumping into relationships, making rash financial decisions, quitting jobs on a whim, or saying things in anger that you can't take back. While gut instincts can be powerful and helpful in some situations, when they're the only signal you're listening to, you're ignoring the checks and balances your head and heart provide.

WHAT IMPULSIVENESS LOOKS AND FEELS LIKE

When acting purely on gut-only decisions, you might experience the following intense, immediate feelings:

- **Compulsion:** There can be a strong urge to act, even if it doesn't make logical sense.
- **Restlessness:** You feel that you *have* to do something right now, or you'll burst.
- **Physical tension:** You may experience tightness in your body, a racing heart, or an adrenaline rush.
- **After-the-fact regret:** Once the initial excitement wears off, you're left wondering, *What did I just do?*

Impulsiveness can also manifest in more subtle ways. It's not always about big, dramatic decisions. Sometimes it's the small, everyday choices that add up over time, like mindlessly scrolling through social media, binge-eating junk food, or procrastinating important tasks in favor of instant gratification.

You might have the following thoughts:

- *I don't know why, but I just have to do this.*
- *It feels right in the moment, so why not?*
- *I'll figure it out later.*

Impulsiveness thrives in urgency. It tells you there's no time to think, no need to process—just act. Wisdom often requires slowing down.

WHEN THE GUT SAYS YES, BUT THE HEAD AND HEART SAY NO

When your gut is the only signal pushing you forward, it feels like an itch you can't ignore. Your head might be listing all the reasons why it's a bad idea. Your heart might be quietly protesting, sensing that this isn't aligned with your deeper values. But your gut is yelling, *Do it anyway!*

A head-heart-gut conflict may manifest itself in the following ways:

- Physical urgency: Your body feels like it's in overdrive. You're jittery, your heart is racing, and you feel like you're on the brink of action.

- Disregard for consequences: You're aware that there might be negative outcomes, but you're convinced you'll deal with them later.
- Overconfidence: You believe you'll handle whatever comes, even if you haven't thought it through.
- Emotional disconnect: You're not considering how your actions will affect your emotions or relationships over time.

You might catch yourself thinking, *I know this is risky, but I just need to do it,* or *If I don't act now, I'll regret it.* But acting impulsively without checking in with your head and heart can lead to bigger regrets later.

JOHN AND THE BATTLE AGAINST IMPULSES

John came to me at max capacity. His schedule was packed, his intensity was off the charts, and his life felt like a whirlwind of activity. But it wasn't just his calendar that was overloaded. He was also at the peak of addictive behavior and pleasure-seeking. For someone so charismatic and strategic, it was surprising how much of his life was driven by impulse.

John's gut was in overdrive. He lived from one impulse to the next, filling every moment with something, whether it was work, social activities, or addictive behavior. But beneath all that noise was a deeper discomfort he was trying to outrun.

In our work together, we focused on slowing down. This was incredibly hard for John because his instinct was to fill every empty space. But as he learned to be gentler with himself, he realized that he didn't need to fill every moment to feel fulfilled. The more he slowed down, the less he needed his vices.

John's journey was more than breaking a habit. It was about learning to sit with discomfort without immediately reacting to it. He discovered that his impulsiveness was a way of punishing himself by never giving himself the time to recover. He constantly pushed himself to do more and was basically destroying himself with pleasure. By confronting those emotions head-on, he began to regain control over his life.

Now, John has entire blocks of time on his calendar that stay intentionally empty. He's happier, less impulsive, and in recovery. By learning to pause and check in with his head and heart, he's found a balance that has transformed his life.

THE POWER OF SELF-CONTROL

The Bible speaks often about the importance of self-control, which means operating with clarity, wisdom, and the ability to pause before acting.

Proverbs 25:28 says, "Like a city whose walls are broken through is a person who lacks self-control" (NIV). Without self-control, we're vulnerable to the consequences of impulsive decisions. Our defenses are down, and we're more likely to make choices that don't serve us in the long run.

Self-control isn't about suppressing your gut instincts. It's about integrating them with the wisdom of your head and the compassion of your heart. When all three signals are aligned, your decisions are swift but also wise and meaningful.

TOOLS TO OVERCOME IMPULSIVENESS AND BALANCE DECISION-MAKING

1. **Pause before acting:** When you feel an overwhelming urge to act, pause. Give yourself a moment to breathe, think, and check in with your head and heart. This simple act of pausing can disrupt the cycle of impulsiveness, giving you space to make a more thoughtful decision.

2. **Implement disciplines and practices:** Create routines that help ground you, whether it's daily reflection, journaling, or mindful breathing. These practices help slow down impulsive tendencies and foster a sense of inner calm.

3. **Seek input and counsel:** Before making big decisions, talk to trusted friends, mentors, or counselors. Getting outside perspectives can help temper impulsive urges and provide valuable insights you might not have considered.

4. **Schedule empty space:** Make room in your life for rest and reflection. When every moment is filled, you're more likely to act impulsively to keep the momentum going. Embracing stillness can help you reconnect with your deeper values and priorities.

5. **Practice gratitude and contentment:** Impulsiveness often stems from a sense of lack or dissatisfaction. By

cultivating gratitude for what you already have, you can reduce the urge to seek fulfillment through impulsive actions.

6. **Develop long-term goals:** Having clear goals can help anchor your decisions and provide a framework for evaluating impulsive urges. When you know where you're headed, it's easier to resist detours that don't align with your vision.

When only the gut is pushing you forward, it's easy to get swept up in the thrill of the moment. But impulsiveness, while exciting, often leads to decisions that don't serve your long-term well-being. True wisdom comes from balancing your gut, head, and heart to make thoughtful, grounded choices that align with your values.

If you find yourself acting on impulse, take a step back and listen to the other signals. Honor your instincts, but don't let them lead you into decisions that you'll regret. By integrating gut reactions with logic and emotion, you'll make decisions that are not only bold but also wise and fulfilling.

Remember, the goal isn't to eliminate impulsiveness entirely. Sometimes, our gut reactions are spot-on and can lead to incredible opportunities. The key is learning to discern when to trust your gut and when to pause, reflect, and consult the other signals.

PERSONAL REFLECTIONS – WHEN ONLY YOUR GUT PUSHES YOU (IMPULSIVENESS)

1. What kinds of decisions trigger my impulsive behavior: financial, relational, or career-related?
2. Do specific people or environments amplify my impulsiveness?
3. What practices or disciplines help me pause and evaluate before I act?
4. Who in my life helps me slow down and think before I make big moves?
5. If I fully trusted that I didn't need to rush, how might my decisions look different?

CHAPTER 12

CONCLUSION: IT'S TIME TO DECIDE

"Once you make a decision, the universe conspires to make it happen."
—Ralph Waldo Emerson

CONCLUSION: IT'S TIME TO DECIDE

IF you've been in church long enough, you've probably heard someone say, "I know that I know that I know." It's one of those phrases that expresses a deep, unwavering certainty. It's the kind of conviction that goes beyond logic or feeling. But what if we took that phrase and gave it a fresh spin? What if "knowing" wasn't just about spiritual assurance but about understanding ourselves on every level—an alignment of our head, heart, and gut?

You've learned how each of these signals contributes to your decision-making. Your head brings logic, facts, and analysis to the table. Your heart brings emotion, passion, and relational insight. Your gut brings instinct, intuition, and quick judgments. When all three are aligned, you can confidently say, "I know that I know that I know." But what about when they're not?

UNDERSTANDING YOUR THREE SIGNALS

The first step in mastering The Decision Code is tuning into your signals. Think of it like learning a new language. You have to listen carefully and practice consistently. When you're facing a decision, ask yourself the following questions:

1. **Head (logic):** Am I overthinking or underthinking? Is my decision based on facts, or am I getting caught up in analysis paralysis? The head signal thrives on clarity, data,

and reason. But it can also lead you into endless loops of doubt if it's not balanced.

2. **Heart (emotion):** How do I feel about this decision? Are my emotions guiding me toward or away from something? Am I flooded or disconnected? The heart is the seat of our passions, but unprocessed emotions can cloud judgment if left unchecked.

3. **Gut (instinct):** What's my immediate reaction? Does something feel off or just right, even if I can't explain why? Your gut operates on instinct and learned experiences, but unchecked, it can lead to impulsiveness.

Pay attention to which signal is the loudest and which ones are quieter. Often, indecisiveness arises when one signal is out of sync with the others.

Pro tip: Consider keeping a "Decision Journal" where you jot down how your head, heart, and gut respond to different choices. Patterns will emerge over time, and you'll get better at interpreting your internal signals.

USING THE DECISION CODE WHEN YOU DON'T KNOW WHAT TO DO

So, how do you apply The Decision Code when you're stuck?

1. **When all three signals align:** This is the easy one. When your head, heart, and gut are all saying yes (or no), trust that alignment. It's a green light to move forward with confidence.

Example: You're offered a job. Your head says it's a great opportunity with solid benefits. Your heart feels excited about the work and the people. Your gut gives you a sense of peace. That's a full-body yes, so go for it.

But what if it's a full-body no? Maybe you're offered a high-paying role, but your head sees the stress, your heart feels no passion, and your gut screams, *Run!* Trust that, too. Saying no can be just as empowering as saying yes.

2. **When two signals say yes, but one says no:** This is where the real work happens. You might have two signals giving you the green light, but one's holding you back. In these cases, the decision is still a yes, but it requires attention to the hesitant signal.

Example: You want to start a new business. Your head has done the research, and your heart is passionate about the idea, but your gut is nervous about the risk. The decision is a yes, but take time to explore that gut hesitation. Maybe it's pointing to something you've overlooked, like financial planning or support systems.

The key here is not to ignore the hesitant signal but to address it. Sometimes, that hesitation is highlighting something that, if resolved, will make the decision even stronger.

3. **When two signals say no, but one pushes you forward:** This is a red flag. If only one part of you is pushing for a decision, it's usually a sign to pause or say no.

    Example: You're considering a relationship. Your heart is all in, and you're infatuated. But your head sees the red flags, and your gut feels uneasy. Even though your emotions are strong, this is likely a no. It's important to listen to the collective wisdom of your signals.

Think of your signals like a three-legged stool. If one leg is missing or weak, the whole thing wobbles. Trusting just one signal without the support of the others can lead to unstable, regrettable decisions.

APPLYING THE DECISION CODE

Let's look at some common life decisions and how The Decision Code plays out in practice:

1. **Career moves:** Imagine you're offered a promotion that doubles your salary but requires relocating to a city you dislike. Your head says yes because of the financial gain, your heart hesitates because you'll miss your community, and your gut feels uneasy about the lifestyle change. In this case, you might accept but negotiate flexible work options or realize the money isn't worth the personal cost.

2. **Relationships:** You meet someone who checks all the boxes on paper because they're kind and successful and share your values. Your head says they're perfect, but your heart feels disconnected, and your gut senses something is off. Despite the logical appeal, this might not be the relationship for you.
3. **Financial decisions:** You're tempted to invest in a friend's business venture. Your heart wants to support them, your gut feels wary about the risk, and your head isn't convinced by their business plan. Here, The Decision Code suggests saying no or, at the very least, proceeding with caution.

PRACTICAL STRATEGIES FOR APPLYING THE DECISION CODE

1. **Pause and reflect:** When faced with a tough decision, take time to pause. Journal your thoughts, emotions, and instincts. This slows down the impulsive urge to act and gives your signals space to surface.
2. **Talk it out:** Sometimes hearing yourself articulate your thoughts helps clarify which signals are influencing you. Talk to a trusted friend, mentor, or counselor to gain perspective. A fresh pair of eyes can often see patterns you might miss.
3. **Test small decisions:** Practice using The Decision Code on smaller, low-stakes decisions. Over time, you'll get better at recognizing your signals and trusting the process.

Try it with daily choices, like what to eat, how to spend your free time, or even which route to take to work.

4. **Revisit past decisions:** Think about past decisions, both good and bad. What were your signals saying at the time? Reflecting on past experiences can help you fine-tune your awareness for the future. Were there moments when you ignored a gut feeling or times when following your heart led you right?

5. **Create space for silence:** Sometimes we can't hear our signals because life is too noisy. Take time for silence, meditation, or prayer. Creating stillness allows your inner wisdom to rise to the surface.

6. **Practice decisional "dry runs":** Before committing to a big decision, pretend you've already made it. How does your head feel about it? Does your heart settle or tighten? Does your gut relax or twist? This mental rehearsal can reveal hidden hesitations or confirmations.

The truth is, you won't always have perfect clarity. Life is messy, and decisions are rarely black and white. However, by understanding your head, heart, and gut signals, you'll navigate the mess with more confidence and peace.

Decisiveness isn't about always knowing the right answer; it's about knowing yourself well enough to trust your process. When you tune into your signals and apply The Decision Code, you'll be more confident in making decisions. Once you do, you'll also be equipped to help others in their decisions. Whether you lead a team that counts on you for guidance or you are raising children who need your direction, The Decision Code can equip you for those leadership roles.

Remember, this is a journey. You'll make mistakes. You'll second-guess yourself. But each decision, whether it turns out perfectly or not, is a step toward greater self-awareness and wisdom. Most importantly, by becoming decisive, you combat the heavy weight of decision fatigue. You cannot eliminate how many decisions there are to make in life, but like any good tool, The Decision Code can help you do what you need to do more easily and sustainably.

Now, as you finish this book and step back into your life, remember that you have everything you need within you to make wise decisions. Trust your signals. Follow the code. When in doubt, pause, listen, and lean into the wisdom that's already there.

It's time to decide.

APPENDIX

UNDERSTANDING YOUR DECISION-MAKING STYLE

APPENDIX: UNDERSTANDING YOUR DECISION-MAKING STYLE

IF you haven't taken The Decision Code Quiz yet, scan the QR code and take five minutes to discover how you're wired. The quiz asks you to rate forty-five statements based on your natural tendencies, not who you think you should be, but how you actually operate when making choices. Be honest about your instincts, even if they surprise you. Once you've completed The Decision Code Quiz and received your personal result, you might be asking: *Now what?*

This appendix is here to help you answer that question.

Each person is wired with a unique order of internal signals. While all three signals matter, the order in which they influence your decisions dramatically shapes your patterns, instincts, and blind spots. Your decision-making style reveals which signal takes the lead, which follows, and which tends to stay quiet unless invited in.

This section contains an in-depth explanation of each of the six decision-making styles. You'll find descriptions of how each profile functions when healthy, where it tends to struggle, and what internal dynamics it must navigate to make wise decisions.

To help make these profiles more memorable and visual, we've paired each type with a chess piece as a metaphor that reflects how that type moves through the world. Some types leap boldly like a knight, while others take measured steps like a king. Some see far and act fast like a queen, while others hold steady ground like a rook. Some types, like the pawn or bishop, reveal surprising influence once you understand their unique path.

The chessboard is about movement, not hierarchy. Every piece has a role. The same is true for you. This isn't a personality box or a behavioral label but rather a look at the way you move through decisions. Learning how you're wired gives you leverage to grow.

Use this appendix as a companion to your journey. Highlight what resonates. Reflect on what surprises you. Move through your decisions with confidence.

♛ THE ARCHITECT (HEAD > HEART > GUT)

You think first, feel second, and act last.

You trust reason over reaction. You want to make sense of what's happening before you feel it or do anything about it. You like structure, logic, and the clarity that comes from slowing things down to think things through. You may care deeply, but your feelings don't always get the first word because your mind does.

You're strategic, thoughtful, and steady. Others may describe you as wise, careful, or insightful. You tend to ask clarifying questions before giving emotional responses. In fact, you sometimes avoid emotionally charged conversations altogether because you haven't finished thinking about how you feel. Your gut is usually quiet until it gets loud.

Imagine someone you care about is upset and wants to talk. You listen attentively but feel pressured to give an emotional response you're not ready to offer. You care about them, but you also need space to process. If you speak too soon, you may regret what you say or say something flat. Later, you write out exactly how you feel in a thoughtful message but by then, they may feel you were emotionally distant.

STRENGTHS

- strategic and thoughtful
- resistant to emotional reactivity
- excellent at building systems and frameworks

- able to remain steady in chaos

WEAKNESSES

- slow to act on internal emotion
- can appear detached or overly logical
- tends to overanalyze or spiral in indecision
- avoids confrontation if emotional clarity is lacking

WHEN YOU'RE UNDER STRESS

You retreat into your thoughts. You may become unresponsive, shut down, or overthink to the point of paralysis. If forced to act before you've had time to think, you may become irritable, overly blunt, or emotionally distant.

WHEN YOU'RE OPERATING IN HEALTH

You communicate your thought process clearly and openly. You give yourself time to reflect and still engage in the moment. You partner your wisdom with care and learn to trust that clarity doesn't always come before connection.

YOUR DECISION-MAKING CHALLENGE

You wait too long to act. Because you want full clarity before making a move, you can miss opportunities. You may also intellectualize your emotions instead of expressing them.

APPENDIX: UNDERSTANDING YOUR DECISION-MAKING STYLE

YOUR DECISION-MAKING HACK

Use a voice note or short journal prompt to process your feelings aloud. Set a twenty-four-hour decision rule. If you still feel the same way the next day, act. Let someone into your thought process even before it's finished. You don't have to wait until you've solved it to share it.

YOUR DECISION-MAKING STYLE ON THE CHESSBOARD: ♚ KING

The Architect is the king: calm, deliberate, and foundational. Just like the king anchors the entire board, the Architect anchors decisions with structure and strategy. The king doesn't rush; it waits until the right time to act. Architects thrive in clarity and measured action. They value order, seek stability, and view missteps as costly. This piece reflects how Architects move through life: methodically, always thinking ahead, building systems before making moves. When protected and empowered, the king (like the Architect) elevates everyone around them.

♛ THE STRATEGIST (HEAD > GUT > HEART)

You think first, act second, and feel last.

You prioritize logic and action. You're a problem-solver who wants answers and results. You trust analysis over emotion and tend to stay calm in chaos. You feel things but rarely lead with feelings, especially when a task or team needs your head and hands.

You're practical and decisive, often stepping into leadership when others freeze. Your gut tells you when to move, but only after your mind makes sense of the options. You value productivity and control. When emotions rise in others, you may feel frustrated, confused, or slow to respond because emotional data takes more time for you to process.

In a crisis, you step up with a plan. You take action, delegate, and organize people to do what needs to be done. After everything settles, someone asks how you're feeling, and you may realize you haven't stopped to consider it. You can describe what happened and what needs to happen next, but your emotional state is still buffering.

STRENGTHS

- clear, rational thinker under pressure
- quick to act when needed
- able to detach from emotion to get things done
- natural leader in chaos

WEAKNESSES

- disconnects from emotional needs
- over-prioritizes action over connection
- may ignore relational impact of decisions
- can become task-driven at the expense of health

WHEN YOU'RE UNDER STRESS

You double down on control. You become hyper-focused on fixing the problem, doing the task, or leading the solution. You may distance yourself from others or get irritated by emotional responses that feel like obstacles to your action plan.

WHEN YOU'RE OPERATING IN HEALTH

You lead with confidence and compassion. You check in with your own feelings before trying to fix everything. You create plans that include people, not just tasks, and you create space for reflection alongside results.

YOUR DECISION-MAKING CHALLENGE

You make things happen but can miss what matters. Because you're so action-oriented, you might solve the wrong problem or push forward without checking in emotionally with yourself or others.

YOUR DECISION-MAKING HACK

Ask yourself: "What does this cost emotionally?" Create pause points before and after a big decision to reflect not just on what you did, but on how it impacted you and the people around you. Progress is more sustainable when it's connected.

YOUR DECISION-MAKING STYLE ON THE CHESSBOARD: ♛ QUEEN

The Strategist is intelligent, resourceful, and powerful. Just as the queen dominates the board with flexibility and range, Strategists blend logic and instinct to cover vast ground. They move quickly but with purpose, often calculating multiple steps ahead. Like the queen, they're assertive leaders who can command a room or navigate pressure with ease. But with power comes responsibility, and this type must guard against overextension and be sure they're moving for the right reasons, not just because they can.

APPENDIX: UNDERSTANDING YOUR DECISION-MAKING STYLE

🧘 THE EMPATH (HEART > HEAD > GUT)

You feel first, think second, and act last.

You lead with compassion. You're deeply attuned to what others are feeling and to your own emotional world. You instinctively want to care, connect, and bring peace. You process decisions through how they will affect others and only afterward consider the logic or the action steps.

You're insightful, warm, and thoughtful. You naturally see emotional undercurrents that others miss. You may hesitate to act too quickly because you want to be sure it feels right. When you do act, it's often from a place of emotional conviction and care.

Imagine you're trying to decide whether to take a promotion. The raise is great, and the role fits your skills but you're more focused on how it will affect your team or your family. You think through how others might feel, and what the emotional ripple effects will be. Only once you've processed that do you begin to evaluate your goals or instincts.

STRENGTHS

- empathetic and compassionate
- emotionally intelligent and intuitive
- deeply relational and loyal
- able to read emotional environments well

WEAKNESSES

- may avoid conflict or hard decisions
- can over-identify with others' emotions
- delays action out of fear of hurting others
- can feel emotionally overwhelmed

WHEN YOU'RE UNDER STRESS

You absorb the emotions of others, even when they're not yours to carry. You may spiral into people-pleasing or feel immobilized by emotional weight. You may seek external affirmation instead of trusting your own boundaries.

WHEN YOU'RE OPERATING IN HEALTH

You hold space for others without losing yourself. You express emotions honestly and clearly while also using logic and discernment to protect your own peace. You trust your empathy without letting it lead you into burnout.

YOUR DECISION-MAKING CHALLENGE

You care so much about the emotional impact of a decision that you delay or avoid making it. You may spend too much time wondering how others feel and lose clarity on what you need.

YOUR DECISION-MAKING HACK

Ask yourself: "What would I tell someone else in my position?" Get clarity by journaling your emotional concerns, then listing your priorities. Use both lists together to make a decision that's kind but not codependent.

YOUR DECISION-MAKING STYLE ON THE CHESSBOARD: ♗ BISHOP

The Empath is spiritual, intuitive, and emotionally aware. The bishop moves diagonally, symbolizing the Empath's ability to see and feel what's beneath the surface. They cut across conventional lines and speak into hearts, not just systems. Bishops often operate from the edges of the board, just as Empaths may prefer to lead from behind or beside. Yet their movement is powerful and far-reaching when fully aligned with both purpose and permission. The Empath, like the bishop, creates emotional clarity and spiritual direction.

♘ THE INTUITIVE (HEART > GUT > HEAD)

You feel first, act second, and think last.

You're emotionally driven but action-oriented. You trust your feelings and instincts and often make decisions quickly based on how something feels in your body or spirit. You process thoughts last, preferring to lead with passion and conviction over calculated reason.

You are expressive, bold, and deeply connected to your values. Others may admire your courage and emotional clarity. You can be spontaneous and creative, but also impulsive or stubborn. When emotions and instincts align, you're unstoppable. When they don't, you can feel torn or unsure of your next move.

Imagine meeting someone new and instantly feeling connected. Before learning about them, you trust your sense of who they are. You quickly make plans or share something personal because it feels right. It's not until later that you think through whether that was wise or not. Sometimes you're spot-on. Other times, you wish you'd asked more questions first.

STRENGTHS

- emotionally honest and expressive
- takes courageous action aligned with conviction
- highly attuned to relational or spiritual environments
- leads with sincerity and passion

WEAKNESSES

- can be impulsive or reactive
- struggles to slow down and evaluate options
- may ignore helpful logic or counsel
- can become emotionally overextended

WHEN YOU'RE UNDER STRESS

You follow your feelings into overcommitment, conflict, or burnout. You may withdraw or explode depending on whether your emotions feel validated. You may later feel regret about how quickly you acted or how emotionally exposed you became.

WHEN YOU'RE OPERATING IN HEALTH

You stay emotionally present while also seeking clarity. You check in with others and create pause before major decisions. You channel emotional energy into creativity and advocacy without losing discernment.

YOUR DECISION-MAKING CHALLENGE

You may confuse emotional clarity with total clarity, which leads to premature decisions. You might also avoid asking hard questions because you've already "decided" based on a feeling.

YOUR DECISION-MAKING HACK

Ask yourself: "Have I considered this from multiple angles?" Wait (even just one night) before big decisions. Process feelings out loud with someone who asks good questions, not just someone who simply validates your first instinct.

YOUR DECISION-MAKING STYLE ON THE CHESSBOARD: ♞ KNIGHT

The Intuitive is creative, surprising, and emotionally guided. The knight's L-shaped move reflects how this type doesn't take the obvious path. They leap over obstacles and often make progress through insight that others can't see. Knights represent non-linear wisdom with the ability to pivot quickly and act boldly. The Intuitive moves through life with feeling and instinct, not formulas. But like the knight, they must stay attuned to timing and trust because not every leap leads forward.

♖ THE ACTIVATOR (GUT > HEAD > HEART)

You act first, think second, and feel last.

You're wired for action. You trust your instincts and move fast. Once you sense something needs to happen, you do it and then think about it and feel it afterward. You value boldness, quick decisions, and measurable results.

You're high-energy, intuitive, and driven. You follow your gut and often get things right on the fly. You don't always need a plan. You just need a green light. But when your impulse isn't checked by thought or emotion, you can come off as insensitive or erratic.

You get an idea, feel excited, and execute it quickly. You're no stranger to booking the trip, launching the project, or confronting the issue. Later, you realize you didn't consider all the logistics or how others might feel. Sometimes it works. Other times, you need to circle back and clean up what your courage forgot to carry.

STRENGTHS

- quick to act and adapt
- trusts instincts and takes initiative
- courageous and unafraid of risk
- good in emergencies or high-stakes environments

WEAKNESSES

- can be impulsive or reactive
- may neglect emotional consequences
- skips planning or analysis
- hard time slowing down or listening fully

WHEN YOU'RE UNDER STRESS

You bulldoze forward. You may overstep, act before thinking, or become irritable when things slow you down. You may ignore feedback, push through resistance, or create unnecessary tension.

WHEN YOU'RE OPERATING IN HEALTH

You still move fast, but with wisdom. You include others in the process and listen to your head and heart before acting. You remain bold without being brash and courageous without being careless.

YOUR DECISION-MAKING CHALLENGE

You decide before you reflect. This can lead to amazing progress or avoidable damage. You may also steamroll others if you don't pause to think or feel.

YOUR DECISION-MAKING HACK

Give yourself a ten-minute pause. When your gut says go, set a short timer to run the idea through your head and heart. Ask yourself: "Does this need to happen now?" If yes, go. If not, wait and plan it well.

YOUR DECISION-MAKING STYLE ON THE CHESSBOARD: ♖ ROOK

The Activator is bold, linear, and action-first. The rook rushes forward in straight lines, clearing the path or crashing through it. Activators, like rooks, are momentum makers. They thrive when there's a clear objective and a short path to execution. But the rook must stay grounded with no diagonals or detours. When Activators resist feedback or emotional nuance, they risk becoming bulldozers. When they pause to check their path, they become champions of progress.

♟ THE INSTINCTIVE (GUT > HEART > HEAD)

You act first, feel second, and think last.

You're driven by instinct and emotion. You respond quickly to the energy of a situation by reading body language, tone, urgency, and risk before most people know what's happening. You don't wait for analysis or spreadsheets. You move when it feels right and stop when it doesn't. Your body picks up signals that others miss, and your emotions either confirm or challenge those impulses.

You're deeply intuitive, though not in a mystical sense. You have an uncanny sense of people, timing, and tension. You often "just know" when something's off or when it's time to act. But because your decisions are driven by sensing and emotion, they may lack structure or long-term strategy. You live in the now, and the now is usually loud.

Imagine you're walking into a meeting and something about the room feels off. You don't know why, but you just know. You adjust your approach mid-sentence or change your presentation style. You lead with energy, vibe, and read of the room. Later someone might ask, "Why did you pivot?" and your answer is, "It just didn't feel right." You might reflect after the fact, but in the moment, your gut and emotions are driving.

In relationships, you're intense and emotionally present. You might have mood swings or be described as "too much" but you're fiercely loyal. You may struggle to explain your needs, especially when emotions override your ability to articulate thoughts. You're not scattered; you're just sensing constantly, and it's a lot to carry.

STRENGTHS

- highly attuned to environment and energy shifts
- decisive under pressure
- emotionally active in real-time
- bold, loyal, and protective of those you love

WEAKNESSES

- can be emotionally reactive or impulsive
- struggles to communicate your thought process clearly
- may neglect logic or data in decision-making
- prone to overextending based on emotion or urgency

WHEN YOU'RE UNDER STRESS

You get overwhelmed by everything at once. You may lash out, shut down, or try to force quick solutions. Your gut keeps moving, your emotions escalate, and your head is late to the game. You may later regret things said or done in the heat of the moment.

WHEN YOU'RE OPERATING IN HEALTH

You move with confidence and compassion. You take time to reflect before acting, letting your emotions settle before your instincts take over. You check in with others, articulate your reasoning, and are more able to course correct without shame. You lead with boldness, but it's grounded, not chaotic.

YOUR DECISION-MAKING CHALLENGE

You react before you reflect. Your instincts and emotions dominate the moment, and your mind arrives too late to help course-correct. This can lead to missteps, misunderstandings, or decisions that feel great in the moment but create cleanup later.

YOUR DECISION-MAKING HACK

Ask someone you trust: "What do you see that I might be missing?" Verbal processing or coaching helps balance your drive with clarity. Use short notes, recordings, or whiteboards to get your thoughts out of your head and into view. Your gut already knows what's next, but your head deserves a seat at the table too.

YOUR DECISION-MAKING STYLE ON THE CHESSBOARD: ♟ PAWN

The Instinctive is humble, reactive, and full of hidden potential. Pawns may only move forward one step at a time, but they can become anything on the board. This style operates from a deep sense of inner knowing, combining feeling with strength. Their journey may be slower, more intuitive, but it's powerful. Like the pawn, the instinctive can be underestimated at times, but when they stay the course, they transform into forces that reshape the entire game.

NOTES

INTRODUCTION

1. Brian Wansink and Jeffery Sobal, "Mindless Eating: The 200 Daily Food Decisions We Overlook," *Environment and Behavior*, 39(1) (2007): 106-123, https://doi.org/10.1177/0013916506295573.
2. Dscout, "How much are we really attached to our phones physically, cognitively . . .?" *Dscout Research Report*, June 15, 2016), https://pages.dscout.com/hubfs/downloads/dscout_mobile_touches_study_2016.pdf?_ga=2.180416224.672 21035.1650551540-199217915.1650551540.
3. Neil Farber MD, PhD, CLC, CPT, "Decision-Making Made Ridiculously Simple!" *Psychology Today*, July 11, 2016, https://www.psychologytoday.com/us/blog/the-blame-game/201607/decision-making-made-ridiculously-simple?utm_source=chatgpt.com.
4. Shai Danziger, Jonathon Levav, and Liora Avnaim-Pesso, "Extraneous Factors in Judicial Decisions," *Proceedings of the National Academy of Sciences*, 108(17) (2011): 6,889–6,892, https://www.pnas.org/doi/10.1073/pnas.1018033108.
5. Baba Shiv and Alexander Fedorikhin, "Heart and Mind in Conflict: The Interplay of Affect and Cognition in Consumer Decision Making," *Journal of Consumer Research*, 26(3) (1999): 278–292, https://www.jstor.org/stable/10.1086/209563.
6. George Weinberg, *The Heart of Psychotherapy: A Journey into the Mind and Office of the Therapist at Work* (St. Martin's Press, 1984).

NOTES

CHAPTER ONE
1. Daniel G. Amen, *Healing the Hardware of the Soul* (Free Press, 2002).
2. Ibid.
3. Ibid.
4. Andrew Newberg and Mark Robert Waldman, *How God Changes Your Brain: Breakthrough Findings from a Leading Neuroscientist* (Ballantine Books Trade Paperbacks, 2010).
5. Jonathon Smallwood and Jonathon W. Schooler, "The Restless Mind" *Psychological Bulletin, 132*(6) (2006): 946–958, DOI: 10.1037/0033-2909.132.6.946.

CHAPTER TWO
1. Ali M. Alshami, "Pain: Is It All in the Brain or the Heart?" PubMed summary; review of Armour's 1991 neurocardiology research, (2019): DOI: 10.1007/s11916-019-0827-4.

CHAPTER THREE
1. Brad J. Bushman, C. Nathan DeWall, Richard S. Pond Jr., and Michael D. Hanus, "Low Glucose Relates to Greater Aggression in Married Couples," *Proceedings of the National Academy of Sciences*, 111(17) (2014): 6,254–6,257, https://doi.org/10.1073/pnas.1400619111.
2. "Lashing Out at Your Spouse? Check Your Blood Sugar," Ohio State University, April 14, 2014, https://news.osu.edu/lashing-out-at-your-spouse-check-your-blood-sugar/.
3. Emeran A. Mayer, "Gut Feelings: The Emerging Biology of Gut–Brain Communication," *Nature Reviews Neuroscience*, 12(8) (2011): 453–466, https://doi.org/10.1038/nrn3071.

4. Joseph E. LeDoux, "Emotion Circuits in the Brain," *Annual Review of Neuroscience*, 23 (2000): 155–184, https://doi.org/10.1146/annurev.neuro.23.1.155.
5. William D. S. Killgore, "Effects of Sleep Deprivation on Cognition," *Progress in Brain Research*, 185 (2010): 105–129, https://doi.org/10.1016/B978-0-444-53702-7.00007-5.
6. Janine Willis, Alexander Todorov, "First Impressions: Making up Your Mind After a 100-ms Exposure to a Face," *Psychological Science*, 17(7) (2006): 592–598, https://doi.org/10.1111/j.1467-9280.2006.01750.x.
7. Anna Richard, Adrian Meule, Julia Reichenberger, and Jen Blechert, "Food Cravings in Everyday Life: An EMA Study on Snack-Related Thoughts, Cravings, and Consumption," *Appetite*, 113 (2017): 215–223, https://doi.org/10.1016/j.appet.2017.02.037.
8. Wendy Wood and David T. Neal, "Healthy Through Habit: Interventions for Initiating & Maintaining Health Behavior Change," *Behavioral Science & Policy*, 2(1) (2016): 71–83, https://doi.org/10.1353/bsp.2016.0008.
9. John F. Cryan, Kenneth J. O'Riordan, Caitlin S. M. Cowan, et al., "The microbiota–gut–brain axis," *Physiological Reviews*, 99(4) (2019): 1,877–2,013, https://doi.org/10.1152/physrev.00018.2018.

CHAPTER FOUR

1. Peter A. Levine, *Waking the Tiger: Healing Trauma* (North Atlantic Books, 1997).
2. Amy F. T. Arnsten, "Stress Signalling Pathways That Impair Prefrontal Cortex Structure and Function," *Nature Reviews Neuroscience*, 10(6) (2009): 410–422, https://doi.org/10.1038/nrn2648.

NOTES

3. Bessel A. van der Kolk, Susan Roth, David Pelcovitz, Susanne Sunday, and Joseph Spinazzola, "Disorders of Extreme Stress: The Empirical Foundation of a Complex Adaptation to Trauma," *Journal of Traumatic Stress*, 18(5) (2005): 389–399, https://doi.org/10.1002/jts.20047.
4. Lisa M. Shin, Scott L. Rauch, and Roger K. Pitman, "Amygdala, Medial Prefrontal Cortex, and Hippocampal Function in PTSD," *Annals of the New York Academy of Sciences*, 1071(1) (2006): 67–79, https://doi.org/10.1196/annals.1364.007.
5. Barry Schwartz, *The Paradox of Choice: Why More Is Less* (HarperCollins, 2004).
6. Leon Festinger, *A Theory of Cognitive Dissonance* (Stanford University Press, 1957).

CHAPTER SIX
1. S. S. Iyengar and M. R. Lepper, "When Choice is Demotivating: Can One Desire Too Much of a Good Thing?" *Journal of Personality and Social Psychology*, 79(6) (2000): 995–1006, https://doi.org/10.1037/0022-3514.79.6.995.

CHAPTER NINE
1. Roy F. Baumeister and John Tierney, *Willpower: Rediscovering the Greatest Human Strength*. (Penguin Press, 2011).

ACKNOWLEDGMENTS

Some things are built with wood, some with steel.
This book was built with people.

Amanda,
You inspire me. You're the reason this book exists. Thank you for the sacrifice you made in your writing and the way you paved for me. Thank you for standing by my side when I couldn't feel, couldn't decide, and didn't know what to do.
All my signals point to you.

Malachi,
My one strong arrow. You're the answer to so many of my prayers. Thank you for cheering me on as I wrote and for making sure I didn't stop having fun. I'll always be here for you in every decision, but I'm not worried about you because you have what it takes.

My friends and family,
You remind me who I am. You keep me grounded. You are the

ACKNOWLEDGMENTS

community I always want to come back to, no matter where my paths take me. I love you all.

My clients,

You are the real authors of this work.

Your stories, your honesty, and your "I don't knows" became the soil this book grew from. Thank you for trusting me to walk alongside you, even when the path was unclear.

The Smith family and all of City of Life Church,

Thank you for a lifetime of paving my way. My interests, my education, my opportunities all trace back to you. I never had a second of fear in this process because I've always felt your strength behind me.

The scholars, scientists, therapists, and theologians whose research I leaned on,

Thank you for giving language to what our hearts and guts often feel long before we know how to name it. Your work built a scaffolding I could climb.

God,

Thank you for the honor to house your work. I'm but a vessel, but wisdom belongs to you. Thank you for the plane ride during which you whispered all this to me.

Anyone holding this book in your hands,
You don't owe me your time. But you gave it. That means more than I can say. Thank you for reading. Thank you for trusting me. Thank you for deciding to allow me into your decisions.

ABOUT THE AUTHOR

Justin McNeil is a pastor, counselor, coach, and fitness instructor with a passion for helping people make wise, courageous choices. At his core, he's a hype man who loves getting loud and will always be willing to match the energy you bring. He holds a PhD in Pastoral Theology as well as a Master of Arts in Christian Counseling from Heritage University and Seminary. He is a Certified Life Coach, Certified Temperament Counselor, and Licensed Pastoral Counselor with the NCCA, and has been ordained since 2007 at City of Life Church.

For almost twenty years, Justin has walked with people in their highest joys and hardest trials and is devoted to equipping leaders, couples, and individuals to navigate decisions with emotional intelligence, spiritual discernment, and daily discipline. His work blends biblical truth, psychological insight, and personal experience, including his own journey through grief and panic disorder, to help others align their head, heart, and gut in the choices that shape their lives.

He and his wife, Amanda, live in sunny Florida with their son, Malachi. When he's not teaching or counseling, you'll find him on a spin bike, floor mat, or winning board games against friends. *The Decision Code* is his debut solo book, offering the framework he has used for years to help people find clarity, confidence, and peace in life's most important moments. He is also the co-author of *Meant to Be: A Devotional for Husbands and Wives.*

RESOURCES FROM THE MCNEILS

The Decision Code: What to Do When You Don't Know What to Do
Overcoming the Overcast: Navigating The Storms of Grief with God
Meant To Be: A Devotional for Husbands and Wives
Grief Journal
Diario De Duelo (Grief Journal)

Available at mcneilcoaching.com/resources

www.ingramcontent.com/pod-product-compliance
Lightning Source LLC
Chambersburg PA
CBHW050107170426
43198CB00014B/2486